About the Author

He has lived in the south of England all his life. Having now reached the grand old age of seventy, he has decided to share his love of poetry with a wider audience. Since retiring, the extra free time has been useful to further this hobby of his.

A Variety of Poems

To Jo and Robin,
All the best
from John H.R
24-5-2024

John Hall-Roberts

A Variety of Poems

Olympia Publishers
London

www.olympiapublishers.com
OLYMPIA PAPERBACK EDITION

A CIP catalogue record for this title is
available from the British Library.

ISBN: 978-1-80439-304-8

First Published in 2023

Olympia Publishers
Tallis House
2 Tallis Street
London
EC4Y 0AB

Printed in Great Britain

A Flower Grown

A flower grows so colourful and bright;
It stretches up to gather in sunlight:
When it dies, its petals will all fall off
To form a soft carpet upon the ground.

On life the flower's given up its lease;
Some people think that flowers signal peace:
When a flower dies, does peace die as well?
And just vanish without even a sound.

To some, peace is a dirty, evil word;
We're s'pposed to live in a sick little world:
A flower can mean harmony and love,
It's peace not war that we should spread around.

People who disagreed would stop and stare
At people who put flowers in their hair:
If all they wanted was for peace to live,
Then was it such a bad idea they found?

A flower grew so colourful and bright;
It stretched up and gathered in some sunlight:
It died, remember those petals that fell?
Remember that soft carpet on the ground?

A Hundred Years Of

Saint Margaret's church has stood here for
A hundred years; and yet
It's always been here for the people;
Never should we forget.

There are times in all our lives when we
Might to a sin be driven:
Allow the fact that we're all human,
Rejoice, our sin's forgiven.

God gave this church for faith and hope,
And peace and brotherly love:
Remember when you pray within,
Each prayer is heard above.

The seven deadly sins show us
Sin is the devil's light:
Come inside and pray to Jesus,
Have faith to know wrong from right.

Under this roof of heavenly love,
Rest from the daily strife;
Christ's love you know it's everlasting,
Heaven's your eternal life.

A War Grave

Her husband was killed in World War One;
But she had been left with a darling son:
She can remember saying to him -
"Hurry up or you'll be late for school;
Breakfast's ready, no time to play the fool."

Off he'd go down the road, and away
To a classroom; so he could learn how to say
His tables, and other important things;
Back home at teatime gives his mum a hug;
Says his tummy hurts, might have caught a bug.

When he left school, he wanted to be
A soldier, like his father, in the army:
She remembers trying to change his mind,
But it was no good; his decision was made and set;
He told her not to worry, not to fret.

The day he left he said his goodbyes,
They both had tears in their eyes;
She felt she wouldn't see him again:
She held him tight, then he was off to war;
She wondered what it was he was fighting for.

She remembers the day the doorbell rang quite loud:
The telegram, the loss, the pain, the feeling proud:
All these thoughts in her mind at the cemetery.
She placed a bunch of flowers on his grave,
Remembering his dear life that he gave.

Though her son has gone she still loves him dear,
She visits his grave many times each year:
A life tragically lost fighting a war;
Does anyone really win when a war is fought?
Is that something young and old alike should be taught?

A Weapon of Mass Destruction

A fighter plane flies low overhead,
While two young children in a cellar hide;
Each parent tries to take some food to them
As bombs are dropped. They don't make it inside.

Panic stricken, the kids both start to cry:
Overhead people die, buildings fall;
Noise from these missiles is so loud.
Only hell can hear frightened children call.

For what seems like an eternity they wait;
Maybe mum and dad will make it, they pray:
At last the bombing stops, the noise abates,
Should they try to leave or should they stay?

Suddenly the floor above them caves in.
Daylight breaks through into their darkest fear;
Eventually they pluck up the courage,
Scarred and bleeding they manage to crawl clear.

They see their parents' bodies on the ground:
Reaching out to hold their hands, oh how they cry;
Up above the air is filled with acrid smoke.
Can anyone explain why they had to die?

The consequence of war can be unpleasant
Inside it all, whoever is to blame;
One thing of which we can all be certain,
Never again will those kids' lives be the same.

Acid Rain Kills

All you see on this old planet
Cannot survive unless we care;
In rain there is a source of life;
Do you love it enough to share?

Rain can make crops grow big and strong;
Acid rain will kill them all dead:
In case you don't know what that means,
Never again will you eat bread.

Know this and remember it well:
If you want to avoid the pain;
Let the sea survive for all sake:
Let clouds survive, life not to take.
Stop the acid getting into rain.

Bullying

A young boy's getting bullied when he goes to school each day;
He's had enough, so this time he decides to run away:
It's cold that night, so he decides to sleep in some old barn,
His parents are both worried sick, they don't know where he's gone.

He wakes up in the morning, he's so frightened and so cold;
He loves his mum and dad so much, something he wished he'd told;
A stranger wanders slowly in and sits next to the boy:
He produces from his pocket a soft and cuddly toy.

He puts his arm around the boy and pulls him to his side:
He hurt the boy who then broke loose and shouted and he cried;
A search party was luckily nearby and heard the scream;
They rescued him and helped to end the nightmare of a dream.

The boy was shaken but unharmed, the man he was
arrested;
It was found that so many boys the man he had molested:
The lad went home to parents who were overcome with
joy,
They'd feared the worst, and thought never again they'd
see their boy.

The man was sent to prison for so very many years,
Because of him so many parents shed so many tears:
It wasn't long before the man was found dead in his cell;
If anyone knew who had done it, nobody would tell.

This story had a happier ending than it might have done;
If he'd told his teachers or his parents, he would not have
gone:
So if you know of anyone who's bullying another,
Don't keep quiet, tell someone, it could be your brother.

COP 26

It's all been said before, so clearly what's the point?
Bang heads together in Glasgow, then disappoint:
The evidence is all around for us to see;
Ice caps melting north and south will deepen the sea.

Planet earth can only take just so much abuse:
It cries out for release from pain, our morals loose;
Ocean life will finish and one day disappear;
But do not worry, we'll all die too, have no fear!

We only have ourselves to blame for what's gone wrong:
Unless we all act now the end won't be that long;
Earth will be dead, devoid of life, and then we find
That for sure it is mankind shall destroy mankind.

Earth Matters

What are we doing to the land?
Wherever you go pollution is found;
Rubbish is thrown into hedgerows,
From a park bench it falls to the ground.

There are landfill sites for materials
And objects that people don't need;
But that broken glass and that metal
Is dangerous, it can cut, make you bleed.

Someone has dumped a car in a field,
It's abandoned and broken and rusty:
A newspaper lies on the summer grass,
It is hot and dry and dusty.

An apple core and banana skin
Are left on the side of the road;
The bin men clear as much as they can,
But even they have a limit to their load.

Of all the rubbish that you discard,
Some will get buried, some will get burned:
It's vital that we keep recycling,
Make sure destruction's tide is turned.

We owe it to all the world's children
To safeguard their future not our past:
This planet can only take so much,
Don't kill it if you want it to last.

The biggest danger to this world
Is really very easy to find;
It's us we should be careful of,
'Cause mankind shall destroy mankind.

Please think before you spread your litter,
Destroying life will cause such sorrow;
For when it's gone there'll be nothing left,
Life and time, they're things you can't borrow;
Not past nor present nor come tomorrow.

For Ever

How many more must lose their life
At the hands of someone using a knife?
That someone can be waiting in sun or shade,
They could no doubt have their hands on a blade.

A young girl on her way home from a class
Sees someone standing near but walks on past;
She's followed to the street where she lives,
And is asked for directions which she politely gives.

Her arms are then slashed, she starts to bleed:
On her suffering the evil one will surely feed.
She's stabbed repeatedly in her neck and back
By someone who's not caring to keep track.

She dies, her suffering's too great to measure;
From it the evil one will gain a sick pleasure.
Her body was found by a small boy walking by.
He went into shock, couldn't move or talk or cry.

The attack didn't happen after dark or late at night.
It took place in the afternoon in broad bloody daylight!
How come no one heard her cry for help or scream?
Do people go about in some sort of a dream?

Isn't it time to stop this mindless evil madness?
Time to prevent all this needless death and sadness
At the hands of someone whom no mercy will show?
The next victim might be someone you know.

Let's purge our society and remove this cancer.
We've simply got to find the answer.
Don't turn away pretending you can't see or hear;
You could be next. Do you want to live in fear?
For Ever?

Found

A loud roar sounded from the cave,
The people trembled with fear;
None of them really felt too brave,
So they never went too near.

When one day a lonely traveller
Arrived in the village from afar;
He found all the residents frightened;
Their fear on the village was a scar.

He decided he wanted to help them,
So he walked to the cave alone;
They all tried to stop him from going,
All he carried was a magic stone.

He reached the cave entrance and stopped,
Placing his stone upon the ground;
Then all of a sudden the stone glowed,
And gave out a very strange sound.

The loud roar from inside soon mellowed,
Then stopped as the monster came out;
It was a most hideous sight
With two heads, and three feet all with gout.

The monster then touched the magic stone,
And in an instant was changed to a man;
The hero had found his lost brother,
And loved him as only a brother can.

Have To

Have to keep a distance from other people:
Have to wear a face mask in a public place:
Have to self isolate with certain symptoms:
Have to sanitise my hands and not touch my face.

Have to cope with a shortage of petrol:
Have to cope with any shortages in shops:
Have to cope with some people pushing and shoving:
Have to endure when one's enthusiasm drops.

Have to hope there's light at the end of the covid tunnel:
Have to accept that normality will never be the same:
Have to plan for the future when all this is over:
Have to – how can we if we've had enough to blame?

Heaven Is ……..

Peaceful and calm, full of harmony,
Soft and gentle, no trouble or pain:
No one is fighting or hurting another,
Peace comes around again and again.

War is finished, killing has ended,
People don't say things that hurt inside;
I remember what life is usually like,
All the pain and suffering, and then I cried.

Forever to be happy all of the time;
No suffering or anguish can be near:
Heaven could be a place here on earth;
We'd have to work for it, so please hear.

Turn to the person who is next to you
To make this place like heaven above:
Remember we're all sisters and brothers;
So why not share with them ….. your love?

How

How can we cook food when the cooker's not working?
How can we make a hot drink without a kettle?
How can we keep warm without heating?
How?

How can we buy food without money coming in?
How can we go out without proper shoes on our feet?
How can we stay safe and dry when the roof's leaking?
How?

How to see a doctor when we can't afford the medicine?
How to call for help when there's no phone?
How to save for our future?
How to die?
How?

If Only

If only we'd treat life as precious,
Fill our time with what is good;
If only mankind could live in peace,
Do unto others as we should.

If only the person next to you
would return your kindness and call;
If only war and violence would stop,
There'd be no need for weapons at all.

If only food was shared out better,
The world has got enough to eat;
If only money could be spent better,
So everyone's life could be more complete.

If only all these things could happen,
Life could be free like a bird up above;
If only you knew you're all my brothers,
Can I share with you all my love?

Journey

He sits on a bench by the station,
It's cold, he's cold, lonely and hungry,
Finds a half drunk cup of warm coffee,
Tastes good, makes it last, time to ration.

Three days with no food in his stomach,
Finishes the coffee, dozes off,
He gets woken up by a loud cough,
He's on the ground laying on his back.

A kind looking gentleman stands there,
Offers his hand to help him stand up,
He looks around for his coffee cup
Was finished, this person seemed to care.

The helper walked him a shot distance,
To a place that was bright safe and warm,
From now on for you this is the norm,
Said to him, giving him a quick glance.

The next morning his body was found
On that bench, look of peace on his face,
At last he'd gone to a better place,
They buried him, no one came around.

Kosovo

A six-year-old boy sits by the roadside on the kerb;
He'd seen his parents and sisters butchered by a Serb;
Before they died his mother and sisters had been raped;
His father tried to call out but his mouth had been taped.

He was all alone and had walked so many a mile;
He'd seen many frightened faces, not one with a smile:
They'd left their villages following a Serb order;
Not everyone would reach safety across a border.

He didn't know where he was or what he was to do;
He'd followed crowds; would he live or die or start anew?
His grandparents had been shot and killed in front of him:
With no food or water his future looked very grim.

The only clothes he had were the ones he was wearing;
He was totally alone, was anyone caring?
He was cold and hungry with no shoes upon his feet:
He entered a refugee camp begging food to eat.

There were thousands of people there all hungry and
scared;
At least here he thought he would find somebody who
cared;
He collapsed with hunger and exhaustion, couldn't stand,
When suddenly an aid worker offered him her hand.

She took him to the first aid tent, hoping to bring him
round;
She didn't know that his parents could ever be found:
She held the boy gently to feed him; oh how she tried;
He laid in her arms, looked at her, closed his eyes – and
died.

Liberation

So many millions passed, so many years too:
Stop crying and trying, don't know what to do;
Can such evil exist? A true hell on earth,
Even give up living for what it is worth.

Hunger, pain, torture, cruelty and such thirst,
Each day they just don't know which one's coming first:
It is such a struggle just to stay alive:
How long to go on? Will anyone survive?

But wait, different soldiers coming, marching here;
Is this truly the end for us? So much fear:
They break the gates open, and to each they stare;
They lay down all their guns, hold out hands to care.

A true miracle has from here rescued all;
They tell us we are free, some so weak they fall:
Soldiers crying seeing the sights of this place;
Hardened fighting men, see the look on each face.

Liberation has come but too late for some:
They have no strength, no feeling, their bodies numb.
They can't believe that they are finally free:
The true stench of death is there for all to see.

Metal Bird

In the middle of the forest high up in the trees;
Its wings flap against high branches slowly in the breeze;
It can become other birds like eagles, kestrels, swans;
Any disguise it chooses, any disguise it dons.

Other creatures are scared by the sound of the monster;
The noise is like a thunderous clap, a violent storm:
Its wings are shiny black, as dark as the depths of the
night;
It casts a shadow on the ground, all are filled with fright.

No one has defeated this hideous thing, not yet;
Like frightened mice the people run and hide for safety;
Fear like a knife cuts through their very souls, but wait!
See!
A stranger, will he save them from their eternity?

No one dared look at the fiery battle that took place;
Man and bird lay dying on the blood soaked forest floor;
With its last breath the bird cries out then it slowly dies;
The man dies crawling to the bird, tears in both their eyes.

My Imaginary World

If all the fighting and the trouble
In the world would stop;
If people had enough to eat
And could harvest their own crop.

If man could think of fellow man
And not just of his ego:
Treat all like sister and like brother,
A treasured friend, amigo.

If we could live in harmony
All over planet earth;
It would be such a lovely place;
We'd know what life was worth.

If all the pain and suffering
In this old world would cease;
If all these things could come about,
I'm sure we'd have – peace.

Passed

He sits on a cold hard concrete step
In a dusty draughty doorway;
Everyone's walking past
Perhaps afraid of what to say;
Hasn't eaten for two days,
Hunger pains in many ways
The will for survival and life
Ebbs further away.

He has no money and no friends,
No relations left alive;
His possessions are in a carrier bag
Letting thoughts of loneliness thrive;
He used to have a house, job and car;
His family was his guiding star
How many years since
They've been gone – five.

Just then a kindly gentleman
Stopped and said hello;
Said there was somewhere
Nice that he could go;
Warm safe and dry with food to eat,
With warm clothes and shoes on his feet,
He made it to the place
He'd hoped to know.

Save A Life

What if -
In a busy crowded shopping centre,
It's in the afternoon, the car park's full;
The local football team's playing at home,
Such a huge crowd that match is bound to pull.

It's also a bank holiday weekend,
The roads are gridlocked, nothing can get through:
Schools are also on summer holiday:
A young boy faints in the heat; what to do?

Mum calls 999 for an ambulance
Which ends up getting stuck in the traffic:
The boy's pulse becomes weak and erratic;
He needs help soon; he's getting very sick.

A paramedic on a motor bike
Is quickly sent to help the patient there;
While examining him the boy's heart stops,
Which means that he needs immediate care.

With an injection and a heart massage,
He manages to restart the boy's heart:
His pulse stabilises, he's gonna live:
His mum breaks down with joy at the new start.

The ambulance arrived shortly after;
The paramedic had saved the boy's life:
The lad recovered, grew up fit and strong;
Got a good job, a family and a wife.

What if – this happened to you?

Save Us Whales

We don't want all the trouble
Being hunted day and night,
It's not our fault that we're so big and scary;
Mankind gets so uptight,
Using harpoons hurts alright,
Those fishermen, all cold and wet and hairy.

If my memory serves me right
There's more sea than land on earth,
But even so we still could live together;
Please leave us all in peace
While we swim the oceans deep;
At least there we're not bothered by the weather.

How would you all like it
If we came up on to land
And started hunting you for all you're worth?
You'd soon get a bit worried,
See a whale up the high street,
You'd probably all give us a wide berth.

You're polluting this old planet,
The land is being spoiled,
You've dumped your toxic wastes into the sea:
You don't need to hunt to kill us,
Just continue as you are,
You'll finish us all off, just wait and see.

When the last one of us dies,
We'll both have tears in our eyes,
No more whale blood or oil to put in pails:
So if you don't want that to happen,
Then you know what you must do;
Act now! Stop the killing! And please save us whales!

School Dinners

Sausages for lunch again,
Chips are cold and soggy;
Hp sauce is right to pour
Over your hot doggy.

Only baked beans turn up hot;
Listen, I want you to know.
Dinners at school were like that
In days oh so long ago:

Now they're really much better;
No more does food turn up cold,
Every meal should taste just great:
Return to the kitchen an empty plate:
Say thank you: isn't that what you've been told?

Spare A Thought For

Winter indoors when you're warm and snug:
Perhaps sitting on the fireside rug:
Or drinking hot coffee from a mug:
Spare a thought for the homeless children.

When you sit down for your Sunday lunch:
Someone's eating crisps, hear them crunch:
Eat cakes and biscuits, have a good munch:
Spare a thought for the hungry children.

When Christmas comes you buy a big tree:
Put presents round for family to see:
Stock up food so you won't go hungry:
Spare a thought for the poor children.

Winter indoors, family's together:
Outside it's cold and nasty weather:
Snow falls upon a robin's feather:
Spare a thought for the cold children.

Planes are flying bombs are falling:
Can't you hear them? The kids are calling:
They hide in fear of pain appalling:
Spare a thought for the frightened children.

What ever is their situation:
Which ever country which ever nation:
They don't deserve this degradation:
Spare a thought for the innocent children.

War, disease, cruelty, hunger, thirst:
Does it matter which one you put first?
Those who suffer that is the worst:
Spare a thought for the dying children.

The Angry Sea

So many people killed, so many buildings destroyed;
The wave from over the ocean has left such a void:
Adults and children alike swept out to sea and drowned;
Where once stood life, now there is death. All razed to the
ground.

Such destruction on this scale is hard to figure.
What would have happened if the earthquake had been
bigger?
Survivors hunt frantically for those missing. It's clear
Their faces show emotions of sadness, loss and fear.

With his bare hands searching through the rubble of his
home,
A fisherman finds his wife's body. Now he's alone.
A young girl cries having lost her father and mother,
Her grandparents, aunts and uncles, sisters and brothers.

No amount of aid can begin to replace such loss:
Orphaned and alone in the world, that's the human cost.
The sea's not angry now. It's calm with blue sky above.
What that girl needs is food, shelter, and a family to love.

The Armada

We're setting sail from southern ports
And heading south for Spain;
We hope to defeat our enemy
And their loss will be our gain.

Though the seas will be rough and cruel,
Sea shanties we'll heartily sing;
We'll fight for our country and honour:
For our wages and our king.

We know that despite our efforts,
We could lose with our armada;
If that is the case we'll try again,
Only next time we'll try 'arder.

So be not downhearted my comrades;
Keep loyal, you know it'll suit yer;
Our battle will be in history books;
And learned about in the future.

The Ones Left Behind

The frightening flood of soldiers
Treating people like rocks and boulders;
Innocent people fleeing for their lives;
Husbands escaping with children and wives.
These people have committed no crime;
Will they make it to the airport in time?
The new government are a ruthless bunch;
After their evil deeds they sit and lunch.

A mother arrives at the airport;
Her husband by the Taliban was caught;
She throws her baby daughter to a U.S. marine;
He understands and nods, she feels serine.
She'll never see her little baby girl again;
Somehow she knows her baby will feel no pain;
But then a miracle, the marine grabs her hands,
reunited with her child on the way to better lands.

Both of them have tears in their eyes;
Get on a plane to take off and fly
To freedom, peace and a better life;
She holds her baby close, been through such strife.
The evil that they've left behind
Will for a long time grind and grind;
Those in charge are bad for that land;
The country will end up a desert sand.

Innocent victims should not be made to suffer;
A peace cordon round the airport could be a buffer;
Stop the panic, suffering, persecution and killing;
Is anyone in that hell hole willing?
These words may end up falling on deaf ears
While the world stands by shaking with fears;
How many more must needlessly die
And end up as stars in the night sky?

At least there they will suffer no more;
Human decency is rocked to the core;
The people behind all this have lasted
For far too long – the evil bastards!

The Real Cost Of War

A small boy so hungry and thin
Sits on the dusty earth hoping for food;
So many others sit around the same place:
They've all fled from war and oppression;
All they have are the clothes they're wearing,
A look of total despair is on every face.

A mother holds her baby daughter
And tries to find scraps of food on the ground:
They're both so weak they've no strength left to cry;
The mother doesn't think there's any hope,
She's lost the will to believe in the future,
She just had to sit and watch her baby die.

A father desperately searches for his son;
They were separated while travelling;
Someone gave him some pieces of bread:
He stumbled into a first aid tent
Hoping to find and feed his only son,
He found him laying on the soil, dead.

All of the refugees in this camp
Were escaping from persecution and fear;
They came because they'd nowhere else to go:
Many will die from starvation and disease,
Alone, cold, tired and hungry with no home:
Ain't this the time for a little peace to show?

All too often innocent people suffer
When fighting breaks out: some will surely die:
Does anybody know what they're dying for?
It's not measured in money, bombs or bullets;
It's the suffering of destruction and death:
That has to be the real cost of war.

Time

Time is so precious not to be lost;
Time must be treasured whatever the cost;
Time can be your friend or even your foe,
Time is a place you can never go.

Time must go on for ever and ever,
Time is the link you cannot sever;
Time can cause hurt and heartache and pain,
Time that is past returns never again.

Time is for real so where does it travel?
Time is a puzzle we can never unravel;
Time is forever whether we like it or not;
Time please don't waste it 'cause it's all we've got.

Vert A La Mer

I saw a light way out to sea;
It stood firm like a rock in the ocean;
Its green reflection on the water
Gave a feeling of calm motion.

The wind increased, the surface choppy:
A gale blew, boats were in danger:
Still that green light stood there, bright and strong:
A friendly sight to any stranger.

The rain came down hard and in torrents;
Hurricane force winds started to blow;
Ships struggled to enter the harbour;
In this weather where else could they go?

In all this one thing didn't change
That seamen were happy to have seen;
The carnage and the violent storm
Didn't stop that light shining green.

W?

Why do so many bombs keep falling?
Where has the daylight gone?
Why are so many suffering?
Where has my family gone?

Why have I no one to turn to?
Will I ever find peace and love?
Which is the path I should follow?
Will I ever feel a white dove?

Will you help me please I can't see?
When will these troubles end?
Why was my sight taken from me?
Why do I not have a friend?

Who is that child calling me?
Why so many a broken heart?
Will they join in our struggle?
Will we ever make a new start?

Wake Up Call

How many more will have to die?
Hunger and pain, no strength to cry:
Dead bodies lay on sun baked sands;
Not enough food grows on these lands.

Politicians talk and discuss:
Somebody asks what's all the fuss?
People still die while you listen;
Talk won't save them. Something's missin'.

The war the violence must cease;
Live can be saved when there comes peace.
Let's all get our act sorted out:
These people need help now! No doubt!

Leaders of governments take heed:
Get off your butts, the hungry feed!
You've all got plenty food to eat:
Nice expensive shoes on your feet.

Think of walking bare foot to live:
You must move so help you can give.
Stop the yakking and start the aid:
Show the world of what you are made.

Help now and stop such widespread death;
Dead can't call for help they've no breath.
Their suffering's like a cancer:
In your strength you have the answer.

War

In a village two children lay dying,
Too hungry and thirsty to walk;
The nearest water twenty miles away,
They are so weak they can't even talk.

They're so thin you can even count their ribs;
Their mother is suffering such pain:
Both her children are close to death now;
The dried tears on her cheeks have left a stain.

They're so dry they've no tears left inside them
Under the glare of the relentless sun,
They cannot feel, they've lost the will to live:
To deserve this, what on earth have they done?

Their mother's now dying from a disease;
Their father was tortured and then killed
In front of them, by soldiers who didn't care
Whose blood they just happened to have spilled.

Their mother now lays dead; and all too soon
Her children will follow her from this place:
With a last drop of energy they touch
Her body, they wipe the stain from her face.

A priest found them huddled together;
Their bodies distorted and so thin:
He choked back tears as he prayed for them;
Could anyone forgive such a sin?

£2000 To Die

A small boat seventeen feet long
Is crammed full with forty-three people:
The boat's owner doesn't know or care that's wrong;
It makes her feel as tall as a church steeple.

The craft sets off, the sea a gentle swell,
Forty-three souls frightened, nervous, scared:
Waves get bigger, storm coming, you can tell;
The boat's captain is drunk, his vision impaired.

Ten miles out to sea a twenty foot wave
Slams the boat broadside, makes it overturn;
Wearing the only life jacket, captain to save;
He rescues a twelve-year-old boy, lesson to learn.

Forty-two perished chasing for a better life;
The boy's parents and brothers dead, he's on his own:
The survivors saved by the coastguard, still alive:
Of the rest no trace, their destiny known.

Arriving in England, the two are safe:
Though suffering from exposure, tired and cold:
The boy collapses, heart attack, and dies,
The captain says the owner should be told.

Gives her address in Holland, armed police call there:
Two thousand pounds per head; she's got her money;
She denies all knowledge, clearly doesn't care;
Shows no remorse in court: finds prison not funny.

Twenty years in jail, is that long enough?
She becomes quiet, inwardly and shy;
Before her sentence ends, she's feeling rough;
With a bit of luck, rough enough to die.

A Brush With The Law

While I was driving the other day,
I saw a cardboard police car;
A cardboard policeman stood by it,
I could tell he was bored from afar.

Five minutes later he overtook me
And signalled for me to stop:
I knew that I had been speeding,
So I accepted it as a fair cop.

He got out and walked towards me
While I wound down my window to speak;
He looked in and asked for my licence,
At this point my future looked bleak.

He said "Do you know you were speeding?
At least eighty miles per hour!"
I thought I had better admit it,
Under the bonnet I did have the power.

I noticed he looked rather pale,
So I asked him was something amiss;
He replied that he just didn't feel well,
And that he wasn't cut out for this.

Alphabet Of Life

A is for all that is decent and good:
B is for bad things avoid if we could:
C is for cuddles exchange every day:
D is for danger make it go away:
E is for everything planet earth:
F is for future for babies at birth:
G is for growing so we get older:
H is for help given by a soldier:
I is for information that we share:
J is for justice that we all should care:
K is for kindred your family is true:
L is for love that they will give to you:
M is for mystery what future holds:
N is for nothing like paper that folds:
O is for other things that we might need:
P is for precious like planting a seed:
Q is for quick before the planet dies:
R is for regret a small child cries:
S is for sorrow child is alone:
T is for time that we spend on the phone:
U is for under where all life will go:
V is for vexation why we don't know:
W is for world that soon will end:
X is for x-ray see what's round the bend:
Y is for you and for all of mankind:
Z is for zloty to refugees kind.

Auschwitz

The train will take you on a journey
To some way away:
You have to go you have no choice
There's nothing you can say:

There'll be no food or drink supply
You will be hungry there:
But when you get off the train
Will someone even care?

You will enter a hut
Your possessions will be removed:
No complaints will be listened to
This has all been approved.

For identification
Numbers printed on your arm:
You will be warm and dry
Don't worry will come to no harm.

Then taken to a large chamber
No windows and one door:
You will probably be wondering
What all this is for.

There is no point in looking up
You cannot see the sky:
Soon you will find it difficult to breathe
Soon you will die.

Man Of The Street

Just down the street there lives a man,
And that's exactly where
He stays; because he has no home,
No bed, no table, no chair.

He'll spend the day just walking about,
Going to no particular place;
Where he comes from nobody cares,
He could disappear without a trace.

Did he have a wife and children,
Friends, a job, a house and a car?
He might have argued with his family,
Which made him want to leave and travel far.

Maybe he is a bachelor,
Or a widower all alone;
Perhaps he has no family at all,
And happiness he has never known.

He might have all his belongings
In a plastic carrier bag:
Too much he thinks how time goes slow;
How life has become one long drag.

When young, he'd probably never had birthday
Or Christmas gifts of sweets or toys;
He'd probably never felt the joy
Of opening presents – just like other boys.

Sitting alone on an old park bench,
He remembered something from long ago:
From way back in his childhood days,
During one winter, while playing in the snow.

He recalls being with his father,
And holding his big strong hand;
His dad said "Wait here son", then walked away:
Although it was freezing, there he did stand.

He waited for a couple of hours,
Then feeling very cold, he walked home;
His mum had left a note saying "Won't be long;
Don't go out or wander or roam."

Several days later. Still alone in the house,
A policeman came to the door.
"Are your parents in?" he asked the boy.
"I don't think they live here any more"

He said in a frightened little voice
To the constable standing by his side
At this point he could not hold back his tears,
He held the policeman's hand – and cried.

The policeman took him to a children's home
Where he stayed for seven long years;
Till one morning – when he was twelve,
He finally realised his worst fears.

His parents had simply abandoned him
When he was just at the age of five;
He never heard from them again,
They had left him alone – dead or alive.

That day he decided to run away
To the only place he knew in town;
The sight that he saw was devastating,
His home and his childhood had been pulled down.

So that was how he came to be
A gentleman of the road:
The unhappy childhood he'd endured
Was to be forever a burden – a load.

Still at least he has his peace and quiet,
Though he often thinks of his father and mother;
His mind begins to wander again,
Thinking "Did I ever have a brother?

Just then a policeman came and asked him
What he was doing in the park:
"Remembering" was his reply;
Suddenly – he blacked out, all went dark.

He had fainted because of his hunger;
Eight days without anything to eat;
It's no wonder he collapsed on the ground:
The policeman stood at his feet.

Then kneeling down by his side, he tried
To restart the beat of his heart;
But despite his efforts to revive him,
He died; his journey to heaven did start.

The cause of his death was starvation,
At least that's what the doctor said;
But I think he died of loneliness,
All those sad memories in his head.

On his tombstone there was an inscription,
It was short and simple and neat:
It contained only seven short words,
"Here lies a man of the street."

Plastic

A lone seagull hovers and lands on the pebbled shore
He's been searching for food – tired – can't fly any more
Struggles to breathe – a plastic straw stuck in his throat
Was dumped overboard with other rubbish from a passing boat

All alone and many miles from his home
The sea is toxic – full of poison and of foam
Has to eat to exist and survive
At the present rate how long to stay alive

After a while he takes off – trying to fly
That plastic straw punctures his lung – surely to die
He bleeds inside – choking on his last breath
A Lone seagull suffers a painful death

How many more wildlife will suffer like this
Pollution in the oceans – all the faeces and the piss
The seas will be stagnant – devoid of all life
A deathly stench will for ever be rife

Plastic Pollution

This then will be the final saga
In the topic of plastic pollution;
Does it have to be science fiction
For mankind to find a solution?

If we don't make so much of the stuff,
There'll be less of it to throw away:
Make only the essential bits:
The world could then have a holiday.

No more wild life choking and dying
With bits of it stuck in their throat:
No more of it floating in the oceans,
Thrown overboard by some passing boat.

Mankind could destroy planet earth,
Mankind could also save it;
No more talking, it's time for action;
Let's cut all the fucking bullshit!

We have it within our power to stop
All this planetary destruction; yet still:
We continue to treat earth like a giant dustbin;
Safe in the knowledge – all life –
We eventually will kill!

Plastic Pollution # 2

Well here we are again,
Mankind ain't got a clue,
Keep screwing up our planet
Like there's nothing else to do,

It can only take a finite amount
Of plastic, rubbish and crap!
Won't find answers on a computer
Or by downloading an app

We talk about space exploration,
To the moon or maybe Mars;
Why not take pollution with us?
Plastic, and hundreds of cars?

Not content with no life on earth
Let's fuck up the milky way
If you feel as strongly as I do
Then have your say.

With luck someone will listen
With luck someone will try
With luck the future might glisten
With luck mankind won't die.

Plastic Pollution # 3

We're still here screwing up our planet
Well with rubbish plastic & greenhouse gases
One day the oceans of the world will come to a stop
Try to walk up to our waist in plastic masses

Why no one listening do we all want to die
We fuck up the land now we fuck up the sea
Maybe that language some people will understand
At least when we all dead we be free

So take this warning and listen good
There is still time to save our life
Cut the shit and cut the waste
Let's cut the crap with a knife

Drugs Abuse

Some young kid sits down in a park,
He's going to stay out after dark:
His widowed mother thinks he's at a friend's,
His father – diving – had died from the bends.

He's meeting someone; he thinks it's good
To buy something he's been told he should:
His best friend told him "You'll enjoy it;
It's ready to use and not in a kit."

At six o'clock a woman arrives,
A four point six litre Jaguar she drives;
She smiles sweetly to help him relax,
He has enough money for two packs.

The woman returns to her penthouse flat,
As far as she's concerned, that's that;
The boy's best friend said "take both it's great."
He did – cause he couldn't hardly wait.

He then decided he would go home,
The streets at night not wanting to roam;
He left the park and started to walk,
Suddenly felt bad and tried to talk.

"Someone please help me – I can't feel my feet."
His legs gave way – he collapsed in the street:
A doctor was called and soon did arrive,
He found the poor lad barely alive.

An ambulance came; the medic did
Everything that he could for the kid.
Took him to hospital double quick,
On the way he was violently sick.

He was in a coma on arrival,
To intensive care – fight for survival;
They called his mother, she came to her son,
Somehow she felt she knew what he'd done.

She held his hand and silently prayed;
Throughout the night at his bedside she stayed:
In the morning when the sun did rise,
She saw him open his tired eyes.

"I love you mum" was all he could say,
She started to cry and looked away;
He gripped her hand and with all his might
Said "I'm sorry mum, please forgive me tonight."

He blacked out then and became very weak;
She leaned over and kissed his pale cheek.
It was his birthday, his age was just ten,
Would she ever take him home again?

He worsened, still beside his bed she sat,
The trace upon his monitor went flat;
Doctors had tried to save him – and they cried;
At nine thirty a.m. that day – he died.

Such a tragic waste – now a young boy's dead,
Someone put sick ideas into his head:
What killed him wasn't flu or germs or bugs,
It was a cocktail of seven different street drugs.

Not like figures on some computer file,
That would be too ugly, inhuman and vile;
He was just a boy feeling pain and pleasure,
His life was what his mum will want to treasure.

Now he is gone and never to return,
He'll never marry, or get a job and earn;
His mother's all alone now – such a shame,
I pray to God you don't end up the same.

Dunblane

A young girl aged five goes to school with her mum;
It's so cold that her fingers are turning numb:
Inside the classroom hangs her coat on a hook,
She's early so she has time to read her book.

The teacher hears a noise like someone knocking,
She doesn't know, the corridor they're blocking:
The noise changes to someone firing a gun;
Children panic, teacher prays what's to be done.

Bullets fly – Children die – teacher now lays dead;
What made it happen? Something somebody said?
Look at those new stars arriving in heaven;
The children won't reach the age of seven.

A madman brought a bloody hell to Dunblane,
Can the town's life ever be the same again?
The pain and tears felt there and further away
Make people sick: they just don't know what to say.

Children murdered in cold blood, and we dither,
Our resolve to right a wrong starts to wither;
Surely we can't do nothing? What happened here
Cannot ever be allowed to re-appear.

The evil that occurred, like cancer, will kill,
Lest we destroy it, so no more blood to spill.
It must be stopped, of that you can be certain,
Or else on life – you can just draw the curtain.

We must be strong and make sure that we all try,
'Cause some will sigh, some will cry, others will die!
Can't you hear the children calling from above?
They're saying stop the killing, start spreading love.

Energy Supply Company

I have tried many times to make contact,
Been kept waiting a long time on the phone;
You just can't fight the big boys, they don't care:
They're happy if you hang on all alone.

The same dreary music twice a minute;
The message saying they will answer soon:
Have they any idea what it is like?
Play something different, just change the tune.

When you finally get through on the phone,
Still cannot get through to them though you try:
An hour's wait, and then to be cut off;
It begs the question, you have to ask why?

How can anybody sort something out?
Bang your head on a brick wall everyday:
So in the end – what the heck – just give up;
There really has to be a better way.

Success eventually might happen;
If you have the strength to keep hanging on:
Problem is not everyone can do that;
Then outside help you must rely upon.

So let this be a warning to us all;
Fair treatment is the least we should receive:
The bigger firms – the harder they will fall;
Perhaps what we need to do is believe.

Like A Bird

The road was as straight as a ruler,
The sky was as blue as the sea,
The sun was as hot as a fire,
I wanted like a bird to be free.

The flowers were as pretty as life,
Birds sang like a sweet melody,
Bees hummed like a dynamo turning,
I still wanted like a bird to be free.

The land was as dry as a desert,
It must have been thirsty like me,
A drink would be like a blessing,
Like a bird I knew I'd be free.

My legs felt as weak as string,
Like a blind man I couldn't see,
Life was always as something precious,
At last like a bird I'd be free.

No more was I dry as a bone,
Fresh air was as sweet as honey,
Nothing was as important as life,
I was free, like a bird, I was free.

Messages

1 Hey pa you borrowed so much money
   To try to give me a better chance in life
   This man can arrange passage to England
   Perhaps one day I can be (for someone) a good wife

2 I'm not sure when we'll meet again
   My journey will be long and hard
   But please don't worry about me
   When I get to where I'm going I'll send a card

3 My water has finished, I'm so thirsty
   I'm hungry too, but hopefully won't be long
   It's dark and cold, we are all shivering
   Maybe I'm being punished for doing wrong

4 We are all talking together to keep going
   It shouldn't be much longer now, I think
   That's a good sign, the container's not moving
   We would all give anything for water to drink

5 It's quiet in here now, only two still alive
   I'm scared, can't breathe properly, I will try
   So cold, can't concentrate, I love you daddy
   It's all quiet now, I'll say goodbye
   Please always remember me
   I don't want to die

Mummy

"Mummy why do we have to go out when it's so cold?"
Crying, a small boy asks, shivering and so frightened:
"That soldier says we must go, but I'll stay with you."
Tying to reassure him she felt his hand grip tightened.

They were put on a train, so many people in a carriage;
She feared she knew their destination, knowledge not to
share:
"Mummy I'm hungry. Have we any bread left to eat?" he
asked.
"We should have some after our journey" was all she
could say.

The train stopped; they looked out; so many people in a
queue;
Realizing where they were, she looked up and started to
pray.
She prayed quietly for her husband and for her only son;
Choking back her tears she knew the truth -
"Mummy why are you crying?"

Numbers

An old couple, they look like they're in their eighties,
Sit quietly on a park bench looking at the flowers:
They have a strangely scared look on their faces;
Perhaps they have been sitting there for many hours.

The weather is hot, but they're both wearing long sleeved
coats;
A young man passes by and says "hello" with a smile:
A trace of a smile appears as they too say "hello",
And would he like to sit and chat for a while.

They sat for ages talking about this and that;
Then the young man saw tears running down their faces:
He asked if they were alright, or perhaps feeling too warm,
Still in their eyes, of fear there were many traces.

He made friends with the couple and arranged to meet
them again;
Asked about their warm coats, did they think sun could do
harm:
With a lump in his throat, the old man pulled up his
sleeve,
And revealed numbers printed on his arm.

A Drunk Driver

Four kids were waiting at a crossing
When a vehicle swerved round the bend;
The driver wasn't concentrating
'Cause he was kissing his girlfriend.

He didn't try to stop in time
And ploughed straight into the children there:
His bumper cut right into their bodies;
There were limbs littered everywhere.

One boy's face was smashed right in,
His skull cracked open on the ground;
His sister's abdomen was crushed,
Her stomach lay spread all around.

The birthday cake she had just eaten
Was soiling her pink party dress:
A boy of four now won't grow up,
His chest was a real bloody mess.

One child survived – a girl aged three,
Her legs were crushed – she'd never walk;
Her mum was with her when it happened,
She went into shock and couldn't talk.

The girl's left arm was completely severed,
She was also blinded in both eyes;
When the police arrived at the scene,
The driver he was then breathalysed.

He was five times over the limit,
The oldest kid who died was seven;
The drunk driver was then arrested
As three young souls arrived in heaven.

The girl who lived was taken to hospital
Where she spent the next two years of her life:
She showed amazing strength and courage;
How'd she coped with all this pain and strife.

The doctors and nurses were all in tears
When her right hand touched her mum's face.
She said "I love you so much mummy".
Of the girl's tears there was no trace.

The driver ended up in prison,
The warning messages he didn't heed.
Why in God's name did he have to make headlines
That four young children will never read?

It's Cold Outside

While walking down the lonely street each evening,
A teenage girl is cold and hungry and tired:
She hasn't eaten properly for two days:
With no money – from her last job – she was fired.

She was mugged – her little bit of cash stolen;
In the attack her coat was damaged and torn:
Her possessions such as they were – also taken -
At times like these – night can blend in to morn.

She finds a large door with a porch way
Thinking to find shelter from the biting cold wind:
Huddling down in one dark and dusty corner
She got cramp in her feet – like they were pinned.

An old newspaper blew in on the breeze,
Wrapping it round her to try and protect from the chill;
It didn't help much – the cold still went straight through -
Shaking and shivering – what was she to do?

She must have dozed off – when woke up felt warm;
Not cold or hungry or thirsty – she cried:
Finally – she had found peace and love -
Finally – she had died.

Radiation Burns

What's that white light – cried people standing there;
They tried to shield their eyes, with despair;
After the bright they could only see dark;
Where were they? At home, shops, or in a park?

Tried to find something familiar they knew:
They could only think that's something they should do:
Everything touched felt hot and burning like acid - - - on
fire
With such a rage – destroying all desire.

What happened to the houses they once called home?
Now piles of burning rubble – destined for ever to roam:
The smell of death and destruction filled the rancid air -
Birds not singing, dogs not barking; was anyone left to
care?

The scars and rashes on their skin grew worse,
From hell to all the world had come a curse:
Now all life on earth is dead – there's no salvation
From the legacy of war with radiation.

Will life ever restart on this burnt planet?
If aliens exist, this rock – they'd scan it,
See total destruction by mankind, nothing left
They'd keep away: earth's infection bereft

Of any hope of survival or of life.
Would anyone willingly take on all that strife?
Till the end of time this planet will be destined to wander
The far reaches of the universe, any future did squander

Seagull

The pebbles on the beach are rolled there by the tide
The breeze is soft and gentle now, waves are not wide
Seagull stands upon the shore – just looking for food
Plenty of fish in the sea – search should be good

Wind becomes a little stronger – hard work to fly
The bird tries to take off, but it can't get too high
Wind becomes a gale – is forced to land upon the sea
Thunder clouds are gathering; will in danger be

Gale becomes severe, the seagull makes it to the beach
Makes it further up so from the sea is out of reach
To storm and then so violent – with dark clouds looming
Rain falls in torrents, thunder is booming

A hurricane now breaks, the seagull's blown on the rocks
Tries to land but can't, and suffers severe knocks
He lies there badly injured, can't make it to the sky
Wings and legs are broken, all he can do is die

After several hours the storm it drifts away
Skies clear, wind gentle, sun shines, looks like a good day
A pair of seagulls searching for their son, then he's found
His lifeless body, battered and bruised on the ground

There's

There's a bird in the sky
It don't want to die
So it flies up high
Perhaps that's why

There's a leaf on the ground
It fell – made no sound
The wind blows it around
Is it lost or found

There's a boat out at sea
Travelling to be free
Is it for you and me
For peace – hear my plea

There's a world full of life
Full of problems and strife
Cuts bad air with a knife
But of good will it's rife

There's start a new trend
Happiness to give – don't lend
Say hello to a friend
For the world – ere it end

Ukraine

Look at those soldiers, weapons and tanks;
Don't know what they're firing, they sure aren't blanks:
Missiles and bombs falling from the air;
Does anyone in the free world care?

We didn't ask for this aggression,
The United Nations has meetings in session;
With N.A.T.O. and others putting sanctions in place,
We pray that they work, not just to save face.

For months he has said no threat of invasion,
The world knows what's happened on this occasion;
Just empty talk, lies and deceit:
He thinks the world will bow down at his feet?

Fact is what he said makes him a liar:
Does that give him the right – his weapons to fire?
If nothing is done he'll get away with it;
Will dig a hole in the ground for democracy to fit.

Who's to say he'll stop with Ukraine?
Next stop Poland, Germany or Spain?
If the cyber attacks are actually the Kremlin's,
Let's hope that the senders get infected with gremlins.

With any war it's the innocent that also get hurt:
Men, women and children – dead – face down in the dirt:
If the world takes measures to stop the killing,
Graves dug in the ground we'd no longer be filling.

Ukraine # 2

I am hiding in my cellar
From that evil little fella,
Our house above is totally destroyed:
Where was once laughter joy and life,
My lovely children and my wife;
Now they're all dead; what's left is just a void.

I didn't ask for all this pain:
There's a bomb from another plane;
When will the noise from those missiles end?
All this dust is making me cough;
The bomb blew half my right leg off;
Has anyone a walking stick to lend?

I will try to leave from this place;
There's nothing left – an empty space;
How long will it take – I must wait and see:
My neighbour has room in his truck;
We'll make it with a lot of luck;
How far have we to travel to be free?

We set off on the bumpy road:
No possessions – lightens the load;
Our progress is slow and fraught with danger:
Explosions can be heard around;
Dead bodies scattered on the ground;
Somebody then flags us down – a stranger.

He says the road ahead is blocked;
A bridge destroyed – the ground was rocked;
Would be better taking quieter route:
So his directions we followed;
By a crater – the ground hollowed;
A soldier stood with gun ready to shoot.

He saw the state that we were in,
Said he could not commit the sin,
Told us the shortest route to get away:
Our truck it then broke down, so near
To the Polish border: we were filled with fear,
Saw Russian soldiers marching all the way.

Both exhausted, we finally fell to the ground;
We then heard an unfamiliar sound;
Offers of help, food and water; could we be?
An aid worker with a friendly face,
Said you have now reached a safe place;
Don't worry or be scared, you're both now free.

Why?

Why do birds fly south for winter?
Why do they search for new life?
Why don't they eat where they're hungry?
Why don't they live where food's rife?

Why do people have to quarrel?
Why do people have to fight?
Why do world leaders argue so?
Why can't they know wrong from right?

Why do children have to suffer?
Why do children have to hurt?
Why are some kids going hungry?
Why are some kids eating dirt?

Why do babies get neglected?
Why are babies left alone?
Why do babies get abandoned?
Why do babies sometimes moan?

Why do families have to split up?
Why do families have to hate?
Why can't families love each other?
Why do they think it's too late?

Why is that tramp on that park bench?
Why has he nowhere to go?
Why should he have to beg for food?
Why is it we do not know?

Why is so much hate in the world?
Why must people live apart?
Why can't we all live together?
Why can't we all make a fresh start?

Why are bad things all around us?
Why must people push and shove?
Why can't we treat time as precious?
Why can't we fill it with love?

Diana

You brought happiness into the world;
The flag of truth you helped to unfurl:
You shone like a star both day and night;
Ignorance you helped put to flight.

Your memory shall live forever,
You're in our hearts, you'll leave us never;
Eternal peace and rest is yours;
You've helped so many a worthy cause.

So goodbye Diana, here's what we'll do,
Till the end of time we'll always love you;
In this life of ours we all play our parts:
But you'll always be our queen of hearts.

Ambience

A lonely man stands by a stream;
His mind – it wanders in a dream;
He sees the water flowing by,
And the reflection of the sky.

The fish swim gracefully along,
Do they know if something is wrong?
The sun is setting – sky turns grey:
The ending of another day.

The trees look different somehow,
He hears the birds stop singing now:
The leaves they fall down from the trees,
They flutter in the gentle breeze.

Something is wrong of that he's sure;
He wonders what he is there for:
What would happen if time stood still?
To live – mankind would lose his will.

People would starve – nothing to eat,
They'd search with nothing on their feet:
His mind returns to when and where
He is; he wonders – was I there?

Don't Fuck With Aids!

He meets a woman in a bar -
Offers to buy a drink;
They quickly start a conversation,
Hardly time to think.

He gives her all the chat up lines,
He must have them on tap:
She says she'll go to bed with him,
But he must wear a cap.

She ends up getting very drunk;
They go back to his place:
Though he doesn't wear a condom,
He still looks her in the face.

A little while afterwards,
Not feeling well one day;
She goes to see her doctor,
Embarrassed what to say.

He takes some samples – does some tests;
Tells her not to worry;
He'll phone when the results are in,
She begs him please hurry.

The results confirm her worst fears,
No cure for her in sight:
She's now HIV positive,
She panics in her fright.

She sees the guy she caught it from;
He clearly doesn't care;
She feels abused and scared and hurt,
And says it isn't fair.

A few months later and she's dead,
A memory that fades;
Let this be a warning to all -
Don't fuck with aids!

Someone Must Pay

That plane is flying low said a passer by,
Hearing the noise and looking up to the sky,
It seemed to be heading straight for the tower,
It crashed there with such a violent power.

The explosion made such a frightening sound,
As many tons of rubble fell to the ground;
So many emergency service personnel
Were crushed and buried in that man made hell.

The other tower suffered the same fate,
People tried to escape – but some were too late,
Some of them did make it – they ran for their lives,
Hoping to see again parents, children, wives.

Hundreds died under the concrete glass and steel,
Nobody could know how the rescuers might feel;
A shoe fell out from under a concrete block,
It still contained a child's foot – in its sock.

So many families destroyed or torn apart,
A widow holds her young son close to her heart;
A father cries out for his teenage daughter,
Has she too been a victim of this slaughter?

A tiny girl is pulled from under a wall,
A rescuer heard her weak voice give a call;
She'd lost a leg and had glass in her tummy,
She started to cry and said "Where's my mummy?"

A policeman held her hands; but soon he felt
Life slipping from her: so by her side he knelt:
As she died he found himself starting to cry,
Why is it so many people had to die?

Yet another plane crashed down to earth,
Passengers tried to help for all they were worth;
To tell the tale nobody was to live:
For all the deaths could anybody forgive?

The Pentagon was also hit by a plane,
So many did not live to work there again;
Death and destruction could be seen on that day
On a scale unheard of – Someone must pay

Uncivil War

A girl is living in a village
All alone – her parents are dead;
She's bought when she's just eight years old
To be a slave – with hard earth for a bed.

She works twenty hours a day
For no money – and only one meal:
She's punished if work isn't done -
How would you expect her to feel?

One month later she is taken ill,
Her owner thinks she is faking;
He takes his anger out on her
With new depths of violence making.

When her body was found in a drain,
It had been badly mutilated:
There were burn marks on her back -
And she'd been viciously violated.

The red cross worker who found her body,
Broke down and cried so many tears;
Gathering the parts in a body bag,
He began to realise his worst fears.

This sort of thing has been going on
For longer than any war has lasted:
Whoever is to blame for this
Must truly be an evil bastard.

He buried her outside a small church,
Prayed while looking to the sky above;
If any good could still exist here,
Why can't it appear as peace and love?

You Cannot Sink A Rainbow

You know that life on earth is in danger;
Overstated? No – not by a long stretch:
Upsetting the fine balance of nature
Can and will kill us after we all fetch.

An eerie hush will fall upon this rock -
No more will birds fly in a clear blue sky;
No clear blue sky will exist any more:
Only greyness will be – to make us cry.

Trees and every living plant life will die;
Scorching deserts will cover all the ground.
In case you don't know what that would look like,
Nothing to see for ever – all around.

Keep on going as we are and you'll see
Animals die a truly evil death:
Rotting flesh – in piles – smells will abound;
Acid rain will stop our lungs getting breath.

In time we will follow and die as well,
Neath the greenhouse gases that cover earth;
Because it's mankind shall destroy mankind.
Over stated? All that this planet's worth?
We must stop trying to sink this rainbow.

STORYLINE
IRELAND

BOOK

Felicity Haye
John McArdle
Sam McBratney
Gerard Woulfe

Oliver & Boyd

Acknowledgements

The publishers gratefully acknowledge the special help and advice of the following in preparing this series for publication: Bernard Brims, BBC Schools Radio, Northern Ireland; Richard Byrne, St Mary's (Boys) School, Navan; Ursula Daly, Educational Company of Ireland; and Tomás Hardiman, Abbey Theatre, Dublin.

We are grateful to the following for supplying photographs and information and giving permission for their use; Aquila Photographics, p53 (foot); G A Duncan, Dublin, pp76 and 77; Richard Mills, p53 (top), p57 (top); N.H.P.A., p60; National Library of Ireland, p23; Nature Photographers, p57 (left, foot); R.S.P.B., p57 (right, foot).

Illustrated by John Blackman, Francis Blake, Mandy Doyle, John Harrold, Tony Herbert, Steve Smallman, Pat Tourret, Barry Wilkinson, Joanna Williams, Jo Worth.

Oliver & Boyd
Robert Stevenson House
1–3 Baxter's Place
Leith Walk
Edinburgh EH1 3BB

A Division of Longman Group UK Ltd.

ISBN 0 05 004043 X

First Published 1988

Set in 14/20pt Monophoto Plantin 110
Produced by Longman Group (F.E.) Ltd
Printed in Hong Kong

Contents

Bert's Mummy

Bert's Daddy worked every day in the shipyard until half-past five, so Bert couldn't go home to his own house after school. He went to his Granny Green's instead and sometimes she was very cross.

Granny Green didn't allow Bert to play in the street in case he was knocked down by a lorry. She didn't allow him to play in the Good Room in case he smashed up one of her china ornaments, and he couldn't play upstairs in Granny Green's because there was no upstairs. She lived in a bungalow.

One day – it was the day when Bert first heard that he was getting a new Mummy – Granny Green played hide-and-seek with him. She couldn't find him anywhere.

"Bert? Where are you? If you are hiding in the Good Room, Bert Green, I am going to *smack*."

"Boo!" shouted Bert. And he jumped out of the big grandfather clock in the hall.

It had been a really super hiding place, but
his Granny Green didn't think so.

"Now look what you've done," she said.
"That clock never stops and now it's not
ticking any more. That clock is very valuable,
it is *not* a hiding place, you bad rascal." And
she added, "I'm telling you, you will have
to behave when your Daddy gets a new
stepmother for you."

A stepmother? What was that, Bert
wondered.

Granny Green had plenty more clocks all over the place, and Bert was glad when their hands showed half-past five. Soon he heard his Daddy's car arriving at the front door.

Bert ran outside, dumped his schoolbag in the back and jumped in after it. Liz was in the car, too. Liz was his Daddy's friend.

"Hiya Bert," she said, "I'm coming to your house for tea and I'm warning you, I'm starving."

Goody, thought Bert. He liked Liz and she liked him. His Daddy said, "I hope you were a good boy for your Granny Green."

"I was pretty good," said Bert, deciding not to mention that he'd stopped the big clock.

Next morning, when Bert went to school with his friends Charlie and Meg, he gave them some important news.

"My Daddy might be getting a new stepmother for me."

Meg knew a lot about stepmothers.

"They can be wicked, you know. Snow White's stepmother gave her poison in an apple and she was horrible."

"It's true," said Charlie, "Cinderella had one who made her do all the work and she got really messed up."

"Because her stepmother didn't love her," finished Meg.

Bert, who didn't know what to say, decided that he didn't want a stepmother after all.

After school Bert and Meg and Charlie came down the path together.

"I see my Mummy," said Meg.

Charlie said, "I see my Mummy."

Bert had a lovely surprise. "I see Liz," he shouted, "she's waiting for me."

Liz took Bert by the hand and they caught a bus into town together. First of all they went to the barber shop because Bert needed a haircut. He could see what was happening in the mirror. Every time the barber did Snip-Snip-Snip with his scissors pieces of Bert's hair fell everywhere and his head seemed to grow smaller.

The barber said to Liz, "Your little boy is

very like you, Missus."

"Do you really think so?"

"Missus dear, that child's your double!"

Liz whispered to Bert, "Did you hear that? The barber thinks I'm your Mummy!"

I wish you were, thought Bert.

Next they went into the supermarket to buy some groceries. They bought a cauliflower and a bag of potatoes at the vegetable counter. Bert chose some packets of biscuits for his school break, and soon the trolley was half full.

"Can I push it?" asked Bert.

"Well all right, but be careful where you go," said Liz, "and push it gently."

So Bert began to push the trolley down the long shop. After a while he forgot that he was pushing a trolley. "Vroom, vroom," he said to himself, gathering up speed, "I'm a lorry driver. Vroom ... "

His trolley bashed into another one, and turned it right over.

"Will you watch where you're going!" said an angry voice. "Look at my groceries – I mean, they're all over the *floor*."

"I am terribly sorry," said Liz.

"I should think so, one isn't even safe in a supermarket any more. Keep your boy under control."

Liz helped the lady to pick up her groceries, then she whispered to Bert, "That woman thinks you're my Bert. Everybody thinks I'm your Mummy!"

I wish you were, thought Bert.

Now, Liz and Bert went into a fishmonger's and bought six silver fish for the tea. The fishmonger wrapped up the fish and handed them to Bert.

"There you are, boyo, six fine Ardglass herrin's. You carry those home for your Mum."

Bert put the parcel under his arm, and smiled. Even the man who sold fish thought that Liz was his Mummy!

When Bert's Daddy came home that evening he hugged Bert and gave Liz a kiss and then they had tea. His Daddy ate three herrings, Liz ate two and Bert had one. He didn't like his fish much because it had too many small bones.

"Daddy," said Bert, "if you get me a stepmother will she make me do all the work?"

His Daddy stared at him with big eyes.

"Who mentioned that you were getting a stepmother?"

"Granny Green. My friend Charlie knows about stepmothers, he says they're horrible and I don't want one."

His Daddy let out one of his big laughs.

"What about Liz – is she horrible?"

"No!" said Bert. Liz wasn't horrible, she was one of his favourite people.

"That's good, because Liz will be your stepmother when she and I get married and she comes to live in this house with you and me."

Bert was amazed. Liz said, "We can do the work together, Bert, if you like – the shopping and the cooking. I can meet you after school some days."

"You'll have to tuck him into bed at night," his Daddy said.

"Of course I'll tuck him in."

"You'll have to tell him stories."

"Oh, there'll be stories. I know *lots* of stories," said Liz.

Bert was happy. He gobbled the rest of his tea, gave Liz a big hug, and ran out to find his friends Charlie and Meg. He wanted to tell those two about his nice new Mummy.

Sam McBratney

Away, Far Away

Sorcha drove the grey cow home at milking time. They took the path through Kylebeg Wood.

The animal knew every turn on the path, so she bustled along. The young girl, however, dallied in the wood.

Suddenly Sorcha was startled by the sound of voices coming from behind a clump of holly. She stepped softly over to the bushes and peeked between the spiky leaves.

Her eyes popped and her heart skipped a beat in amazement at the sight that met her eyes. Ten tiny people, in old-fashioned clothes, sat in a circle in a small glade covered with bluebells. They were not much taller than the bluebells.

Sorcha stood there spying on them, safely hidden from their view.

One of the tiny ladies stood up and danced along the glade until she found a dandelion clock. She plucked it and brought it back to

her companions. Then she stood in the centre
of the circle and puffed at the clock to send the
downy seed-carriers floating away on a breath
of air. When the dandelion-head was bare, she
chanted a verse:

"*Dandelion, dandelion,*
yellow and bright,
Trundle me, bundle me
right out of sight.
Like the sweet bluebells, I cannot stay;
So chase me, and take me away, far away."

No sooner had she said the last word than she was gone. In the twinkling of an eye she had vanished.

One of the little men then stood up, blew a dandelion clock and spoke the words. He too vanished. The others followed, one by one, and in the end Sorcha was alone.

The cow had long since gone from the darkening wood and was probably in the shed by then. Sorcha's mother would be annoyed that the girl had not tied the animal in her stall and put hay in the manger.

But Sorcha put thoughts of mother and manger out of her mind.

She plucked a dandelion clock. Then, standing in the bluebell patch, she blew away the feathery seeds and recited the fairy chant.

"Dandelion, dandelion, yellow and bright,
Trundle me, bundle me right out of sight.
Like the sweet bluebells, I cannot stay;
So chase me, and take me away, far away."

The world went dark, and Sorcha's head was full of flashing lights and jangling sounds.

This lasted for just a little while. Then her head cleared and the wood and the bluebell glade were gone.

She was in a cool, dark room without windows. A thin line of daylight showed beneath a door. As her eyes got used to the half dark, she saw that she was in a large pantry. Around the walls there were shelves, full of bread, vegetables, jars of jam, honey, preserves, crocks of flour and meal, plates of cakes and fruit, and bags of oats and rice; enough to feed a small army.

The door opened and in came a young girl wearing white cap and apron. When she saw Sorcha, her eyes and her mouth opened wide. She screamed, a long, sharp scream.

Immediately she was joined by an older lady and a man. The man caught Sorcha's arm and dragged her out of the pantry.

"We've caught you at last," said the woman. "So you're the little thief who has been stealing our food."

"No! No. You're making a mistake," Sorcha

pleaded. "I've only just arrived here. I've never been here before."

"And how did you get into the pantry, young lady?" the man asked. "We were in the kitchen all morning. You couldn't get in there unknown to us. Did you get in by magic?"

"Yes," Sorcha said. "I did."

"Ah ha, so you tell lies too," the woman shouted at her. Then she turned to the girl in the white apron and said, "Get the mistress at once. The master too. They'll hear about this."

16

When the master and the lady of the house arrived, they quizzed Sorcha.

"Where have you come from?" the lady asked.

"Kylebeg."

"I've never heard of it," the master said. "Where is it?"

"In the County Clare."

"Good heavens, girl, that's in Ireland. How did you get across the sea, and then from the coast to here?"

"I just chanted a fairy spell and suddenly I was in your pantry."

"A likely story!" the lady of the house said mockingly. "Put her to work, Cook, and don't spare her."

"Very well, madam," the lady replied.

From that moment Sorcha's life was a misery. She was driven from her bed before the dawn, and, from then until late at night, she worked like a beaver. She cleaned out fireplaces, set fires, brought fuel. She washed floors and clothes, vegetables and dishes. She swept the kitchen and the yard. She fetched and carried from kitchen to garden to parlour to laundry. She laboured for master and mistress, for cook and butler, for parlour and chambermaid, for housekeeper and gardener. And for her pains she got hard words but no thanks.

But Mary, the girl who found her in the pantry, became her friend. They shared a tiny bedroom at the top of the house. There, every night, before they fell asleep, they chatted in whispers.

One evening, when they had gone to the bedroom, Mary burst out, "I saw them today. I saw them!"

"Who?" Sorcha asked.

"The fairies. Your friends. I saw them, and they spoke to me."

"You're joking."

"No. I was in the west pasture and there they were. In a hollow, and I was almost upon them before I saw them. I was terrified."

"What did they say?" Sorcha asked.

"They said, 'Tell Sorcha she must break out and come to this place. Tell her she must go back the way she came. The spell must be changed.' Then they said something I didn't understand. They said it several times."

"What was it?"

"Something like 'This hill, down hill, do.' "

"This hill, down hill, do," Sorcha repeated slowly, trying to puzzle out its meaning.

"Oh, they said it much faster than that," Mary told her.

"I don't know what it means. Maybe I'll find out when I go there," Sorcha said thoughtfully.

Late the next afternoon she stole out of the house and found the hollow in the west pasture. The grass was thick there and dotted with buttercups and thistles.

Sorcha thought over the words the fairies spoke to Mary.

" 'She must go back the way she came,' they said. That must mean that I should chant the spell again."

She did so, but nothing happened.

"They said, 'Change the spell'. Yes! Of course! I have it. There are no bluebells here, just buttercups."

So she said the spell again, but changed it slightly:

> *"Buttercup, buttercup, yellow and bright,*
> *Trundle me, bundle me right out of sight.*
> *Like the sweet buttercups, I cannot stay;*
> *So chase me and take me away, far away."*

Again nothing happened.

"Oh, what kind of a head have I?" she scolded herself. "I didn't blow the dandelion clock. But there are no dandelions here, only thistles and thistledown."

Then suddenly the strange words that Mary heard came to her.

"Oh, we are stupid," she laughed. "It was not 'this hill down'. It was thistledown. That's what they were saying. 'Thistledown will do.'"

She closed her eyes for a few minutes as she tried to make a new verse. She took a globe of

thistledown, pinched off the down and blew it away on the breeze. She chanted her new spell:

> *"Thistledown, thistledown, fluffy and white,*
> *Trundle me, bundle me right out of sight.*
> *Like the sweet buttercups, I cannot stay;*
> *So chase me and take me away, far away."*

It worked. The world went dark for a few minutes. Her head was full of flashing lights and jangling sounds.

When her head finally cleared she was back at home, in the cow shed. There was her mother, milking the cow.

"Sorry I'm so late, Mammy," Sorcha said to her.

Her mother dropped the bucket and spilled the milk in surprise.

"You scared me," she said laughing, and she threw her arms around Sorcha and hugged her. "Where have you been for the past two days, child? The whole countryside has been looking for you!"

Gerard Woulfe

Johnnie Dunlop on bicycle with early pneumatic tyres, 1888.

Riding On Air

John Boyd Dunlop wrapped an extra piece of
canvas around a bulge in the tyre and put a
little melted rubber over it. When the rubber
cooled the bulge was not as bad as it had been.
Dunlop would have liked to repair another
bulge on the other side of the wheel. But time

was running out and Willie Hume was telling him to hurry.

"It'll do," Willie Hume said. "I have to be off to the cycle track."

"I hope you win," Dunlop said.

"Nobody gives me a chance," Hume said. "All the du Cros lads from Dublin are competing."

"Who are they?"

"You mean you don't know who they are?" said Willie Hume in disbelief.

"Never heard of them," Dunlop said.

"They're the seven sons of Harvey du Cros. He was boxing champion of Ireland and founded a rugby club called Bective Rangers. The sons are all great cyclists – all champions."

"All seven of them?"

"Yes. Wouldn't it be nice if an ordinary little Belfast man could beat them. Nobody in Dublin has ever heard of Willie Hume."

A gleam lit Dunlop's eye. "That would be nice," he said.

"And I've been trying out this pumped-up tyre of yours," said Willie. "It goes much faster than the solid rubber tyre. It's lighter and it bounces. That makes it speed along more quickly. I think it's a great invention."

"Oh, I don't know," said Dunlop. "It's a bit of fun, I suppose. I had fun inventing it."

Outside Dunlop's workshop, Willie Hume put the bike into a rubber-wheeled cart and headed across the city. When he arrived at the cycle-track the du Cros boys were already there with their shining bicycles with thin solid rubber wheels made specially for racing. All eyes were on them. The crowd hardly noticed any of the other riders. Almost all the riders were lined up for the start when Willie Hume came out with his bicycle to join them. Hardly anyone noticed him until a boy began to laugh and point at him.

"Look at the bike with the funny wheels," the boy said. The crowd turned towards Willie and began to laugh.

"His tyres are going to have pups," one man said, and a roar of laughter went up from the crowd.

"Look, his tyres are all bouncy and jumpy," someone else said. Some cheered to add to the fun.

"He'll get sea-sick from bouncing up and down," another shouted. Willie Hume didn't mind.

"We'll see who's laughing at the end of the race," he said to himself. He lined up for the start.

The du Cros boys were away first and for lap after lap of the track they took turns at leading so that the leader could break the wind for the others. Willie Hume kept close to them, bouncing along on his inflated tyres, the people laughing each time he went past them. Their laughter soon stopped however. They began to realise that this unknown from Belfast was keeping in touch with the most famous riders in the country, tucked in behind them and still looking strong.

As the race went on and there was no sign of Hume falling back, the laughter turned to cheering for the little man on the bike with the bulging wheels.

"I hope the tube doesn't burst or something," Hume said to himself as he bent

lower over the handle-bars and pedalled with
all his might. A great cheer went up as he
passed the youngest of the du Cros boys
and before long there were only four of them
in front of him; Harvey Junior, Arthur,
Frederick and William. Hume pushed on
harder and, as he did, the du Cros boys went
harder still.

Lap after lap they sped around, their tyres raising dust from the track as the spring breeze began to dry it out. Soon Hume was level with Harvey Junior's back wheel and, with a strong thrust on the bend, he was past him. Three more to go and already they were wilting. If only the tyres would hold out. He looked at the back one. It was bulging a little more, he thought, the bulge going around as the wheel turned. Suppose they burst now! He put the thought from his mind quickly and pedalled on. The strain of pushing the heavier solid tyres was now beginning to tell on Arthur

du Cros, and Hume caught up with him and passed him.

The other two weren't giving in however. They pedalled for all their might, panting, puffing. Hume kept after them doggedly. Two laps to go and he was still behind but closing the gap quickly. As they began the last lap he was on their heels and then, going down the back straight, he passed Frederick du Cros and only William was in front of him.

Hume was almost exhausted, air pumping into his lungs, his heart almost bursting, his back and legs aching. But he put everything he had into one last effort. On the last bend William du Cros's bicycle skidded a little and Hume passed him on the inside and was heading towards the finishing line. The crowd could not believe their eyes. They gasped, cheered and then roared him on, jumping up and down with delight and admiration.

As Hume crossed the line such a roar went up that it could be heard far and wide. Hume stopped his bicycle and turned to go back towards the crowd. As he turned he saw an elderly man with a trilby hat and a flowing white beard coming towards him. The old man was excited and waving his arms in the air.

"Wonderful! Wonderful! A marvellous achievement!" said the white-bearded man.

"Thank you."

"Wonderful. I don't wish to take from your own performance but that tyre is really something."

"I know it is. But I didn't invent it. The inventor is a man called John Boyd Dunlop."

" I'd like to meet him," the man said. "I think it's the tyre of the future. I'd like to talk to Mr Dunlop about starting a factory to make thousands of them. In no time we'll have every bicycle in the world using tyres like that."

"I'll tell Mr Dunlop that."

"Can I come around to see him?"

"Yes, I'll arrange that," Willie Hume shouted above the noise of the cheering crowds. He wrote out Dunlop's address and handed it to the hatted man. "But Mr Dunlop himself says it'll never come to anything. He says it was good fun inventing it but that the only use anybody could have for it is for racing."

"I'll prove him wrong," the bearded man said. He put Dunlop's address in his pocket and pushed his way through the jostling, chanting people. "In eleven years it will be 1900. And I can tell you: by that time we will have the world riding on air."

"Who will I tell him you are?" Hume shouted.

"I'm Harvey du Cros," the bearded man said. "And those fine brats you beat to-day were all my sons. The best of luck to you."

A look of joy spread across Willie Hume's face. He couldn't wait to get back to the inventor to tell him what du Cros had said. But he knew only too well that John Boyd Dunlop would only laugh and say that some men could be very foolish.

John McArdle

Bad Temper

Eithne was in a bad temper. For the third morning in a row she'd been late down to breakfast and Mummy was very cross with her. Eithne hated being scolded. She sat down at the kitchen table feeling hot and shouting at Mummy inside her head.

Then she found that her little sister Ita had finished the cornflakes. The last bowl of cornflakes was Eithne's favourite. It was all ground down like sawdust and it soaked the milk up as soon as you poured it. Eithne had been looking forward to that bowl of cornflakes all week.

"Ita, you've taken my cornflakes. That's mine and you're eating it."

"It is not yours."

"It is so."

"It's not, it's Mummy's."

"You know I always have the sawdust."

"Then you should come down in time to grab it."

"You knew I wanted it."

"Why should you always have it?"

"It's mine."

"Well, I've got it now, so sucks."

"You're not to say that. Mummy said you weren't to. Mummy, Ita said sucks."

"Rotten old tell-tale."

"I am not a rotten old tell-tale, you rotten little thief."

"MUMMY, Eithne called me a thief."

"Children, what is all this noise? Eithne how dare you start this nonsense after what I said to you just now?" Mummy had come in from the hall and she was *very* angry. Eithne was so miserable she couldn't even speak. But Ita was furious now and she banged her spoon on the table.

"Mummy, Eithne called me a thief."

Mummy got so cross with Eithne that she wouldn't hear another word. Ita was bundled into her anorak and sent to play with Brian and Jane next door. And before she knew what to do or say, Eithne had been given some toast and marmalade, which she hated, and sent out into the garden to do some weeding.

"And I don't want to see you again before lunchtime," called Mummy as she shut the back door.

"Well, I never want to see you again as long as I live," muttered Eithne. She didn't mean it. But it made her feel a bit better to say it.

Eithne hated weeding. The path was gritty under her knees and slimy with snail tracks. The clay got under her nails and the roots of the dandelions wouldn't come out properly. She dug her fork into the earth as hard as she could and found she had pulled up a great, wriggling worm. It made her feel sick.

Soon she was hacking and slashing away at the weeds without even looking at what she was doing. Even though it was a horrible, damp day she was getting hotter and hotter. She couldn't even open her coat. Mummy had looked so cross when she'd buttoned her into it. Eithne thought she'd better just keep it on.

"I hate everyone," she muttered, and

scrubbed a filthy hand across a filthy face.

She screwed up her eyes and dug her fork
into the flowerbed. With one giant heave, she
uprooted another weed. Then she stopped
in horror and gaped at what she'd done. It
wasn't a weed she'd uprooted. It was one of
Mummy's flowers. It was a thin, green shoot
with little, green leaves growing from it.

If she had been watching what she'd been
doing she'd have known at once that it wasn't

a weed. But now she'd pulled up one of Mummy's flowers and Mummy'd be crosser than ever.

A big lump suddenly rushed into Eithne's throat. Her face got hotter and hotter and redder and redder. She closed her eyes and opened her mouth and burst into tears.

"Eithne, pet, what's the matter?" Mummy crouched beside her. She put her arm around Eithne's shoulder and hugged her tightly. Eithne pushed her face into Mummy's neck like a baby and howled.

When she was able to speak again her voice was funny. She kept gulping whenever she tried to take a breath. But at last she explained what she'd done.

"I've pulled it up and now it's going to die and it was one of your flowers and I didn't mean to." She gulped again. Mummy hugged her.

"Of course you didn't mean to. It won't die, I promise you. Not if we plant it again quickly."

"I didn't mean to kill it," said Eithne. Her nose felt very big and her eyes felt very small. "I lost my temper."

Mummy was pushing the roots of the little green shoot back into the earth.

"It'll be grand now," she said. "It'll never know the difference." She looked at Eithne.

"I tell you what," she said. "Would you like to have it for your own? Then you can look after it yourself. Will that make up for uprooting it by mistake?" Eithne rubbed her nose on her sleeve and nodded.

So for weeks afterwards she watched and cared for the little green shoot and watered it when it was dry. It grew higher and higher and thicker and thicker and stronger and stronger each day.

Then, one morning when she went to look at it, right at the top Eithne found a flower. It was a round, yellow flower with a flat, brown centre as big as a cornflake bowl. She had grown a sunflower.

Felicity Hayes-McCoy

Mrs McCarthy's Dumplings

Once upon a time there was a little village that stood in the twist of a road that curled around a mountain. And in that village was a school for boys. It was run by an old man called Mr McCarthy. He was a good teacher and the boys were happy enough with their lessons. But there was one thing they weren't happy with. And that was the food. Mr McCarthy's wife did the cooking. And she was a dreadful, awful, horrible cook.

For breakfast she would make porridge. And the porridge was full of little, hard, slimy bits that turned to little, dry, flakey bits when you sucked them. And she would fry sausages. The sausages were all black and burst on one side and all red and raw on the other.

For lunch she would make soup. The soup was all full of knobbly bits and hairy bits. And she would make stew. The stew was full of stringy bits and gristly bits. And she would

make dumplings. They were worst of all.

Mrs McCarthy's dumplings were as heavy as stones. Nobody could ever eat them. Every Wednesday she'd serve them up, two for every boy. And every Wednesday they'd sit there until they were as cold and as hard as a plateful of cannonballs. And then she'd take them away and slice them up with a sharp knife and serve them for tea in sandwiches.

Then, one day, a wild, green dragon came to live in the mountains. He was a great, big, fire-breathing dragon with green scales and yellow teeth and sneaky, stupid eyes. Ranting and raging, he was out all hours, seeking whom he could devour.

He devoured a whole football team in the lane behind the parish hall one night. No-one ever found the football again either. He devoured two old women outside the village shop when they'd just bought food for a week. Their families were left very sad and very hungry. He devoured a big, fat farmer who was leaning over a gate looking at a field of lambs. And he devoured the field of lambs into the bargain.

The people got so worried that they offered a reward of three bags of gold to whoever would rid them of this wild, green dragon. But nobody could. Because as soon as anybody tried to, the wild green dragon would devour him. And that would be that.

And so the weeks went by until one day one of the boys at Mr McCarthy's school had an idea. The boy's name was Myles. The day was Wednesday and Wednesday was dumpling day.

On that Wednesday Myles waited until dinner was over and the other boys had gone into the yard. And then he whipped every one of the dumplings that were left on the table into his school satchel. And he ran away up the mountain to where the dragon had his cave.

Then he called out to the dragon to wake him.

"Are you in there, dragon?" said Myles.

"I am," said the dragon. And up he jumped

with his green scales clattering like old tin cans. So Myles took hold of his satchel by its long, leather strap and swung it round and round above his head.

Out came the dragon with his jaws wide open for his dinner. And Myles took careful aim and shot his satchel full of Mrs McCarthy's dumplings down the dragon's throat.

With a gulp and a choke that brought tears streaming down his scaly cheeks, the dragon swallowed the lot. So there he was with twenty four of Mrs McCarthy's dumplings like a load of lead in his stomach. Suddenly he didn't feel at all well.

He tried to snarl fiercely. But it sounded strangely like a burp.

"Er, pardon me," said the dragon.

"Don't mention it," said Myles.

"Look, I'll devour you in a minute," said the dragon. "I've just got a couple of things to do inside first." And he crawled very quickly back into his cave.

So Myles went back down the mountain and he was sitting at his desk in time for his next lesson.

That night there was a howling and a roaring from the dragon's cave that kept everyone up till four in the morning. So next day they went up to see what had happened. There lay the wild, green dragon with his four legs stuck up in the air. He was killed stone dead by Mrs McCarthy's dumplings.

The people were delighted. And so was Myles when they gave him the three bags full of gold. He spent them all and gave a party. He bought hot, sizzling sausages and smooth, scrambled eggs and brown, crusty rolls and yellow pats of butter. With heaps of beans on toast. And he bought chocolate puddings and apple tarts with nuts and brown sugar. And he bought green grapes and red grapes and pears and pineapples. And every boy at Mr McCarthy's school had as much as he could eat.

But there was one dish that Myles never touched again as long as he lived. And that was dumplings.

Felicity Hayes-McCoy

Something to Remember

"I have a blackbird, a thrush, a robin, a jackdaw, a sparrow, and four others." Joe Flynn reeled off the names like a song.

"What are the others?" Des Ryan asked.

"I'm not telling."

"Why not?"

"Because I want to win. And if I tell you, you'll go there and get them too, and then I won't win."

"Meanie!" said Owen McCarthy.

"What have you got, Billy?" Jackie Walker asked Billy Condon, the youngest of the group.

"I have a jackdaw and a sparrow."

"And – ?" Jackie encouraged.

"That's all."

The others laughed.

"You haven't much of a chance of winning with those," Owen McCarthy told him.

"Where have ye got all those birds?" Billy's Uncle Matt asked.

He was sitting in a deck-chair beside where the boys lay on the lawn. They thought he was asleep because his eyes had been closed for half an hour.

"We've only got them in our notebooks," Joe Flynn answered. "When we see a bird, we make notes about it in our notebooks, and then we go to our bird books and find out what it is."

"What was that young fellow there talking about winning?"

"The teacher is giving a prize when we go back after the holidays," Joe said.

"A pair of field-glasses," Owen McCarthy butted in.

"It's for the best bird-watcher," Joe continued.

"And how is the teacher going to decide who that is?"

"You get a certain number of points for every bird you have," Jackie Walker explained. "A small number for the common birds that we see every day, and then higher points for birds that aren't seen so often."

Later, when the others had gone, Uncle Matt asked, "Would you like to win that prize, Bill?"

"Not half," Billy answered. "But I haven't a chance. The birds I see are always gone before I can get a good look at them."

"That's because you don't stay still when you are watching them. If you want to find some rare ones and score high points, you should come fishing with me. The river is a great place for birds."

"When are you going?" Billy asked eagerly.

"I'll go on Saturday if I can borrow a car. I'll call for you early, so be up."

Saturday morning was fine, and the whole family got up early. They were sitting at breakfast when they heard a frightful racket in the road outside the house. A car had come snorting and banging to the front door, and the horn was loud enough to wake the dead.

Billy ran to the window.

"It's Uncle Matt," he shouted, "in a car."

The others joined him at the window.

"A car!" Dad laughed. "You mean a heap of scrap metal."

It was an old car. The body was crumpled. The mudguards were loose, jogging up and down as the engine ticked over. The roof was gone, and in its place was a piece of floor lino with an all-over pattern of red roses.

"Are you coming?" Uncle Matt shouted as Billy and his parents came out.

"May I, Dad?" Billy asked his father.

"In that?" Dad asked, raising his voice in surprise.

"It's all right," Mother said. "Matt knows a lot about cars."

"Come on, boy. Jump in," Uncle Matt said.

"I'll get my notebook and my bird book," Billy said as he ran into the house.

For over an hour they chugged slowly westward, over the flat land – cornfields, trees, green pasture dotted with black-and-white Friesian cattle.

Then they began the slow climb up

Lyre Hill. The land was different there. Not many trees, just a few spruce or pine for shelter around farmhouses. Isolated holly bushes. Rocks broke ground in the small fields, and sheep nibbled the short mountain grass between the rocks.

At the top of Lyre Hill Uncle Matt stopped the car.

"Look!" he said. "There. Perched on the telephone pole."

"What is it?" Billy asked, excited.

"Go on. Put it in your notebook. You must find out what it is. No cheating."

"Brown bars on the chest," Billy said aloud, so that he would remember it all when he wrote it down. "As big as a jackdaw. Long tail. Brown back. Brown wings. Curved beak. Bright yellow eyes."

"That's it. Now find it in your bird book," Uncle Matt said as he set the car moving again. They freewheeled down the western side of Lyre Hill.

"I have it," Billy shouted. "It's a sparrowhawk."

Jackdaws

Sandmartin with young

"Very good," Uncle Matt laughed. "That should be worth a few points."

At the bottom of the hill the road ran beside the Glashadoun River. The river bed was rough, strewn with large boulders, and the water was loud as it tumbled over the smaller rocks and swirled around the larger ones. The banks were walls of solid rock in great rounded humps and hollows worn smooth over the centuries by the passage of the stream.

Uncle Matt took his fishing tackle from the boot and was soon sitting on a flat rock and casting his line over a wide dark pool.

Billy wandered along the bank, looking for birds. It was a beautiful place, and he enjoyed every minute he spent messing about on the bank. He threw off his sandals and paddled in the shallows. In deeper pools he saw trout like dark torpedoes slipping by in the clear water. Now and then there was a plop as one came up to grab a fly, and, when Billy looked around, only ever-widening rings on the surface showed where it had been.

By midday he had added five names to his list. Sandmartins, brown with white breast, pointed wings and forked tail, flitted in and out of a hole in the face of a sandbank.

In a still pool a tall, grey heron stood, its long beak like a spear at the ready, a wisp of limp black feather hanging like a pigtail at the back of its white head. It was the biggest bird Billy had ever seen, as big as their Christmas turkey.

On a bramble twig he saw a yellowhammer, bright yellow but with its back and tail streaked with brown.

Then he heard a sound like two pebbles striking together. The sound continued and he traced it to a small bird on a thorn branch. It had a black head, a chestnut breast, brown back, and white collar and wing bar. This was the stonechat.

Standing on a rock in the middle of the stream was a busy little bird. It was blue-grey above and yellow underneath, and had black and white streaks on its wings. All the time its tail kept bobbing up and down, up and down. Billy had to check the name a few times because in spite of the bright yellow under parts, it was called the grey wagtail.

Then on a low flat stone, just at water level, he saw a dipper, brown with a large white apron. It was nodding its head non-stop.

"Time to put on the old feed-bag," he heard Uncle Matt calling. "Get the stuff from the car."

Billy brought the bag from the boot. When he came to the bank, Uncle Matt was already building a fire on the flat rock.

First he laid down a bunch of dry grass. Then, with a penknife, he pared shavings from an ash stick, letting them fall on the grass. Over the shavings he placed thin dry twigs, and over them he built a wigwam of thicker sticks.

He lit the grass. A few thick braids of smoke curled upward, and then there was a spurt of orange flame. This was followed by another flame and then several flames dancing between

Yellowhammer

Stonechat

Heron

the leaning sticks until the fire was blazing brightly.

When the tea was made, they sat on the flat rock, eating and chatting about the birds Billy had seen. But for the most part they ate in silence, listening to the splashing of the water and now and then a short burst of birdsong from the fields.

"Don't move," Uncle Matt said quietly.

Billy stopped chewing on his sandwich.

"Now be careful. Don't move a muscle. Talk if you wish but don't move. Is that clear?"

"Yes."

"Now don't move your head. Just turn your eyes to the left and look."

Billy almost shouted with joy. There was the most beautiful bird he had ever seen in his life. It was stopped in mid-air, about ten feet above the water. Its wings fluttered so fast that they were just a blur. It was most brightly coloured, all blue and flame: blue in the upper parts and fiery orange underneath.

Its long black beak moved to left and right as its eyes searched the water below. Then, without a hint of warning, it dropped like an arrow. There was a light splash as it hit the water. In an instant it came up again and sprang into the air, its beak now holding a wriggling minnow.

Then it was gone. Suddenly, like a blue bullet it shot downstream.

"Now, put that in your book, young man," Uncle Matt told Billy. "Not many of your friends will have that fellow."

"What is it? What is it?" Billy asked him excitedly.

"That was a kingfisher. Write down in your book that you saw this bird at 13.30 on the eleventh day of August, 1987, on the banks of the Glashadoun River in the townland of Curramore in – "

"Why should I write all that?"

"Because you might never see one again, and it is something to remember."

"I might win those field-glasses."

"You might at that," Uncle Matt said. "You might indeed."

And he did.

Gerard Woulfe

Kingfisher

Orla's Secret

Orla liked lessons. At school she sat by the window. Her best friend Ann sat beside her. Ann and Orla were best in the class at drawing. They worked together on a big picture of the playground. It was to hang on the classroom wall.

One Monday morning Orla felt very strange. She had a funny feeling in the back of her throat. Her head was hot and her feet were cold. Mummy said she was to stay in bed until she was well again. For three days Orla felt sick. She couldn't read her comics. She didn't want her dinner. Then, on Thursday, she felt better. And on Friday she got up. She had missed a week of school.

On Monday she was glad to be back. Ann had nearly finished the picture without her. Orla coloured in the trees. Then it was ready to hang on the wall. They were very proud of it.

One thing had changed in the classroom. The clock on the wall had broken. After break, the teacher asked for someone to go and see the time on the clock in the hall. Everyone wanted to go. They sat up straight and put their hands in the air. Everyone except Orla. Orla couldn't read the clock. The others had learnt when she was sick at home.

Orla put her head down on the desk. She hoped the teacher wouldn't see her. Ann was sent to find the time. The lesson went on. But now Orla had a secret.

She was afraid to tell the teacher that she couldn't read the clock. She knew it was silly not to tell. But she couldn't help it.

Next day someone had to go and find the time again. When the others put up their hands Orla felt hot all over. She dropped her crayon. Then she bent down to look for it. When she looked up again, one of the boys had gone out to the hall.

All day long Orla felt terrible. She wished she had told the teacher yesterday. Now she was afraid that everyone would laugh at her.

Next day Orla didn't want to go to school. But she wasn't sick so mummy said she must. At playtime she hid behind the bicycle shed. Ann found her by the wall. Ann had been watching her.

"You can't read the clock, can you?" said Ann.

"Yes, I can," said Orla.

"No, you can't," said Ann. "I've been watching you."

"I don't care," said Orla.

"You do care," said Ann. "Look, I'll show you. It's easy."

Ann picked up a stick and drew a clock face

on the gravel. By the time the bell rang Orla
felt better.

That afternoon Ann and Orla drew lots of
clock faces. Each one showed a different time.
Soon Orla could read them. It wasn't hard at
all.

The next day the classroom clock was
mended. No-one had to go to the hall to see
the time. The teacher never knew that Orla
had been so silly. And Ann never told Orla's
secret.

Felicity Hayes-McCoy

Me Myself

Once there was a farmer called Conn who
went out for a walk. He walked and he walked
until he came to the edge of a deep, black lake.
Then, suddenly, he heard a fierce, loud roar.
Out of the lake jumped a big pooka and a little
pooka. And they pulled him down to their
cave at the bottom of the lake.

"Sit down there and don't move," said the little pooka to Conn. So Conn sat down.

"Now you sit down in front of the door," said the little pooka to the big pooka. "You can keep your eye on him.

"And I'll go and boil some water," said the little pooka. "And we'll have him for the dinner."

The big pooka sat on a stool in front of the door. He looked at Conn. Conn felt very small. He looked at the big pooka. The big pooka looked very big.

But though pookas were very big and pookas were very black they were also very stupid. And Conn knew this. So he thought of an idea.

"What's your name?" said Conn to the big pooka.

"Never you mind," said the big pooka. "Never you mind what my name is. What's yours?"

"Oh, my name's Me Myself," said Conn.

"Is it?" said the big pooka. "Well, you just sit there, Me Myself and we'll have you for the dinner." The big pooka yawned a big, black yawn. And then he fell asleep.

Conn looked at the big pooka's stool. If he could just push it over a little he could get out of the cave. But would the big pooka wake up?

He pushed a little. Then he pushed a little more. Then he pushed a little too much. And the big pooka fell off his stool and bumped his elbow on the floor.

"OOOoo, Ooo, Ooo, I'm hurt," roared the big pooka. In came the little pooka with a spoon in his hand.

"Who's done what to you?" said the little pooka.

"I'm hurt, I'm hurt, me elbow's hurt," roared the big pooka.

"Well, who hurt it?" said the little pooka.

"It was Me Myself hurt it," roared the big pooka.

"Well, in that case I've no time for you," said the little pooka. And he went back into the kitchen.

The big pooka sat down on his stool. And

then he yawned another big, black yawn. And he fell asleep again.

Conn looked at the stool. If he could just push it over a little he could get out of the cave. So he tried again.

He pushed a little. Then he pushed a little more. Then he pushed a little too much. The big pooka fell off his stool. And this time he bumped his other elbow on the floor.

"OOooo, Ooo, Ooo, I'm hurt," roared the big pooka. In came the little pooka with a cup in his hand.

"Who's done what to you now?" said the little pooka.

"I'm hurt, I'm hurt, me elbow's hurt," roared the big pooka.

"Who's hurt you?" said the little pooka.

"Me Myself hurt me," roared the big pooka.

"Well, in that case I've no time for you," said the little pooka.

"But it was ME MYSELF," roared the big pooka.

"Don't I know it was?" howled the little

pooka. "And I've no time for you at all. I'm trying to get the dinner."

"But it was ME MYSELF," screamed the big pooka. And the little pooka threw the cup at him.

That started it. The big pooka threw his stool at the little pooka. Then the little pooka threw a pot of jam at the big pooka. So there they were, screaming and howling and roaring and throwing things.

While they were at it, Conn walked out of the cave. He swam to the top of the lake. He shook the water out of his coat. And he was safe in his own home in no time.

Felicity Hayes-McCoy

The Curtain

Kate spent all of Sunday waiting for Monday.
On Monday night she and her best friend
Esmé were going to the theatre. Kate had once
seen a puppet show. Esmé had been to a
pantomime. But on Monday night they were
going to see a real play, at the Abbey.

Kate's dad worked at the Abbey. He was a
stage manager. Kate didn't know a lot about
what a stage manager does. But she did know
one thing. Her dad was in charge of the
curtain. And that made him very important.

After school on Monday, Esmé and Kate
went home to Kate's house for tea. Kate told
Esmé everything she could remember about
the theatre. "It's called the Abbey Theatre
and it's in a street called Abbey Street," she
said.

Esmé was brushing her hair in front of the
mirror. "Will we see your dad on the stage?"
she asked.

"No, silly, he's not an actor." Then

Kate remembered a good word. "He'll be backstage," she said. "That means behind the scenes."

Kate's aunt, Emer, drove them into town. They parked in a multi-storey car park. Then they walked to the theatre. When they got close to it, they saw that there were pictures and posters outside. They had lights around them.

Esmé read out the name of the play. Kate looked at the photographs. Then Emer pushed open the big, glass doors and they went in. Outside it had been dark and cold. Inside it was full of light and very warm.

Crowds of people stood about talking. Some had programmes in their hands. Some were meeting their friends.

Esmé nudged Kate. "See those people waiting over there?" She said. "That's the box office. They're waiting to buy tickets. We stood for ages for tickets for the pantomime."

"Well, we don't need to wait tonight," said
Emer. "Kate's dad gave me our tickets. Let's
find our seats."

The seats were numbers five, six and seven.
They were in row J. Kate found the row
marked J first. Esmé found the seats with their
numbers.

They sat down and looked at the stage. It
was covered by a big, blue curtain.

All around them, people were coming in and
sitting down. Men at the doors checked their
tickets. People were laughing and talking.

Emer opened a programme. Kate looked at
the list of names on the middle page. She
nudged Esmé. "Look, there's dad's name."

Esmé read it out, "Stage manager, Paul
Cox. Who are all the other names?" she asked.

Kate stuck her nose in the air. "Just actors,"
she said.

Suddenly they heard a gong. The lights
began to go down. Programmes rustled.
People coughed. Then there was silence. As it
got dark, the heavy curtain slid out of sight.

"That was my dad," whispered Kate to Esmé.

And there was the stage, shining and bright in the centre of the darkness.

The play was wonderful. In the interval, Emer took them upstairs to the bar. She had coffee and Kate and Esmé had orange. Everyone talked loudly.

Then they were sitting in the dark again, waiting for the curtain to go up. And Kate could hear her heart thump in the silence.

When the play was over, everyone clapped. The actors bowed again and again. The curtain came down, cutting out the light. Everyone clapped louder. The curtain went up. The actors were smiling.

Kate and Esmé clapped till their hands were sore. Then Kate's dad brought the curtain down for the last time. The light on the stage was gone and it was all over.

Felicity Hayes-McCoy

Welcome to the Abbey Theatre

The first Abbey Theatre was opened on 27th December 1904. It got its name from the street on which it stood – Abbey Street.

On the 17th July 1951 after a performance of a play called *The Plough and the Stars*, there was a terrible fire. The next night although costumes and scenery had been destroyed, the play went on in the theatre next door.

In 1966 the New Abbey Theatre was opened. The first play to be acted there was *The Plough and the Stars*.

The new theatre is really two theatres in one building. The big one is the Abbey and the small one is the Peacock.

The company of actors who perform plays in the Abbey Theatre are known as the Abbey Players. There are about twenty other people who are employed at the theatre – stage managers, lighting and sound operators, designers, wardrobe staff and people who sell tickets, and many others.

People go to the theatre to see different kinds of plays. Sometimes the play is new and is being performed for the first time. Plays first seen at the Abbey are now seen all over the world. The famous play *The Plough and the Stars* was first seen at the Abbey Theatre.

The New Abbey Theatre

Foyer of Theatre

Inside the Theatre – ready for a performance of "The Plough and the Stars".

A Tall Story: The Ears that Emigrated

Now here is a true story about Cathy
Robinson's ears. She wanted them pierced,
you see. Every day she tortured her mother,
saying, "I'll run away if you don't let me. All
my friends have their ears pierced."

So her mother agreed. Cathy had her ears
pierced.

The ears didn't like it. They jumped into
the washhand basin when Cathy was cleaning
her teeth and objected in the strongest possible
terms.

"How would you like to have needles
shoved right through you?" said Right Ear.

"Filled full of daylight," said Left Ear.

"We're emigrating," said Right Ear.

Cathy closed her eyes and finished cleaning
her teeth without looking. Was she imagining
things?

She was not. When she opened her eyes,
Left Ear said, "We are going to live with your

friend Sylvia Small, she knows how to treat ears properly."

"Sylvia Small has short hair," Right Ear said, "Sylvia Small is proud of *her* ears."

So saying, they emigrated together, pausing only to wish Cathy good luck in the future.

Cathy shouted for her mother and father and her two brothers, and they all ran to Sylvia Small's house in the next street.

Sylvia was surprised by the sudden fuss. Why did everybody suddenly stare at her and madly wave their arms?

"What's wrong?" she said sharply. "Anybody would think I had two heads to see you all!"

Sylvia did not know yet what a good guess this was – she now had four ears instead of two. When she looked in the mirror, she screamed and fainted clean away.

Nobody knew what to do, this sort of thing had never happened before. A neighbour said they should call the hospital or the fire-brigade. Sylvia recovered from her faint,

rushed to the mirror, and saw that she still had four ears.

"Dial 999," she roared, and passed out again.

This happened twice more, and each time Sylvia woke up, she screamed blue murder because she had twice as many ears as she ought to have.

Cathy's ears got fed up with the din and saw that they had made a bad mistake.

"We don't like Sylvia Small," they said to Cathy, "she's a noisy person. Can we come home again, please?"

Cathy said, "Yes, you can."

Those ears had learned their lesson and gave no more bother. And that story is as true as there's rain in Ireland. Why else do you think Cathy Robinson keeps her hair short and always wears light wee ear-rings?

Sam McBratney

Wonderful Oliver Sundew

Do you see that person standing on the back of a frog? That's Oliver Sundew. This story tells you how Oliver became a tooth-fairy.

It was market day in Oliver Sundew's home town. Mr Nimble Jay was about to make a speech from the balcony of the Town Hall. However, the place was so crowded and so noisy that nobody could hear him.

"Now listen to me, all you people," he said loudly and crossly, "I have some news. *Important* news, so be quiet and listen!"

And he glared at them all – especially the Fiddler, who was making more noise than anyone else. The crowd fell silent.

"That's better," said Mr Nimble Jay. "I'm here to tell you that a tooth has just come out in a place called Newcastle in County Down. It's a top tooth, a front tooth, the very best sort you can get, and so we are sending a team of tooth-fairies to bring it back. What do you think about that?"

The crowd was delighted. Everybody loved the excitement of a tooth-hunt, so it was hardly a surprise when dancing broke out all over the tooth-cobbled square. Hats flew in the air and the Fiddler lifted his violin to his chin and played more loudly than ever. Oliver Sundew stood on his frog's back and cheered until he was hoarse.

When at last a hush fell over the market-place, Mr Nimble Jay was able to continue. "Four of us will leave to bring back the tooth. But remember – this is going to be dangerous."

"Aaaa!" said the crowd.

"If *you* want to be chosen to come on my tooth-hunt, bring yourself to the Town Hall tomorrow morning. Do not apply if you are afraid of magpies, spiders, earwigs . . . "

"Ooooo," sighed the crowd.

". . . Or anything else that gobbles fairies up. Tomorrow morning, nine o'clock. And don't be late."

And that was the end of Mr Nimble Jay's

speech. Oliver Sundew climbed on board
his frog and rode home in such a state of
excitement that he was trembling all over.

"I'm not afraid of magpies or spiders,"
thought Oliver. "If I go to the Town Hall
tomorrow morning, maybe Mr Nimble Jay
will pick me to go and get that tooth!"

When Oliver arrived at the Town Hall early
next morning, there was already a long queue
waiting to see Mr Nimble Jay. Oliver saw two
of his friends. One was called Cornpepper
Rose and the other, Henry B.

Cornpepper Rose said, "Hiya, Olly."

Henry B said, "Do you want to be a tooth-
fairy, too?"

Then another voice spoke. It belonged to Martin Goosegrass. "What are *you* doing here, Oliver Sundew? Nimble Jay will never pick you to be one of his tooth-fairies. He would rather go on his own than pick *you*."

"He'll maybe not pick you either, Martin Goosegrass," said Oliver.

The queue began to move. Soon it was Oliver's turn to go in and see Mr Nimble Jay, who was a burly-looking fellow with a big, red face. He wore a boiler-suit, a bowler hat, and a pair of rubber boots with the tops turned down.

Mr Nimble Jay leaned over to inspect Oliver Sundew.

"So. You want to be a tooth-fairy, boy."

"Yes, sir," said Oliver.

"Are you afraid of spiders and beetles and creepy-crawlies like that?"

"No, sir."

"Scorpions, then? What about jumping trout and the Kingfisher Blue?"

"Well I don't like them very much," said

Oliver, "but I'm not afraid of them."

"Good. Can you fly fast?"

Oliver Sundew paused. As a matter of fact he couldn't fly at all well.

"You see, sir," he explained, "I flew into a candle when I was small and I've only got one good wing."

"Then you won't do!" declared Mr Nimble Jay. "You just won't do. What would happen if you got chased by a wasp?"

Oliver didn't know what to say. "What would you do if you were chased by a blasted robin or a jenny wren? They'd eat you. Gobble you. Peck, swallow and whoosh – no more Oliver Sundew. Sorry, lad, until you've got two good wings you'll just not do as a tooth-fairy."

Naturally, Oliver was very disappointed. "I'm a very good swimmer, sir," he said.

"Swimming's no good," cried Mr Nimble Jay. "But there is something you can do for me. Run over to the bank across the square and get me a coin. Tell the bank manager it's for a front, top tooth in perfect condition."

So Oliver Sundew hurried across the tooth-cobbled square to the bank. The manager wore a stiff white collar and at first he looked down his extra long nose at Oliver.

"Hmm. An Irish tooth, eh?" said the bank manager, turning to a huge map of the world behind him. "It might be bad, you know. Those children eat so many horrible sticky sweets. We don't pay much for a *bad* tooth, you know."

"This is a perfect tooth," said Oliver, "it has no fillings."

"Then I suppose I shall have to give you a fifty-pence piece. Oh well."

A few minutes later, Oliver Sundew came out of the bank with a 50p coin so bright that it dazzled the eye, and so large that he had to wheel it along like a hoop.

Already the square was bustling with activity, for the tooth-hunt was about to begin. Flags were flying, and the Fiddler played lively tunes in the street. When Mr Nimble Jay arrived, Oliver was pleased to see that his friends Cornpepper Rose and Henry B had been chosen to go on the tooth-hunt.

Then he noticed somebody else. Martin Goosegrass was going, too. No doubt this was because he could read maps and fly very fast, even in the pouring rain.

"I told you so, Oliver Sundew," said Martin Goosegrass nastily. "I said Nimble Jay would never pick you, and I was right – you're just not the proper sort to be a tooth-fairy."

It was almost time to go. Mr Nimble Jay, Cornpepper Rose, Henry B and Martin Goosegrass rose into the air, and beneath them, suspended in a large net, the sparkling coin swayed to and fro.

The crowd began to shout.

"Be careful!"

"Watch out for spiders' webs."

"Don't fly near the telephone wires!" cried
Oliver Sundew.

He was feeling quite sad, so he jumped on
his frog's back and hopped home.

"I can't read maps very well," thought
Oliver as he bounced along under the
hawthorn trees. "I can't fly very fast and I'm
not really much good at anything, except for
swimming. Toads alive, I should have been a
fish!"

The hours went by. In the tooth-cobbled square, crowds began to gather. They waited anxiously for news of the tooth-hunt.

Soon, terrible rumours began to spread. Some said that an owl had gobbled Cornpepper Rose for supper. Others said that a cat had caught Henry B.

"I hope it isn't true," thought Oliver Sundew, who was just as worried as everyone else.

And then suddenly, amid a great stir of excitement, Martin Goosegrass flew into the market-place and held up his hand for silence.

"We can't get it!" he told the crowd breathlessly, "we just can't reach the tooth. It's way down deep in a glass of water – you never saw a tooth in so much water in your whole life!"

The crowd let loose groans, sighs and other noises of dismay. Fire, oil and water – these were the things which fairies hated most.

Martin Goosegrass spoke again. "Mr Nimble Jay sent me back for somebody who is not afraid of deep water.''

That silenced the crowd completely. None of them could bear the thought of wet wings – most of those fairies refused to fly in a shower of rain.

Then one voice spoke up clearly.

''I'm not afraid of water. I'll get the tooth.''

Martin Goosegrass turned to face the speaker. He could hardly believe his eyes. It was Oliver Sundew.

''You? But you've only got one wing.''

''I've got one wing and a half,'' Oliver corrected him, ''and I can fly a bit. In fact I can fly a lot if I take rests. And I can swim.''

Somebody shouted from the crowd. ''He's right, you know, I've seen him. By the toads, he can swim better than a tadpole. Oliver Sundew is the only chance we've got.''

So they told Martin Goosegrass that Oliver was the one he must take back with him, and Martin Goosegrass was afraid to argue with so many people.

''Well you'll have to be quick, Oliver

Sundew," he warned. "People will be waking up in about three hours time."

And Oliver knew what *that* meant. If a human being saw a fairy, that fairy vanished. Nobody knew why or where to, but the thought of being seen by an early-morning milkman was enough to make a fairy shiver until his wings fell off.

Away they went. Oliver flew as quickly as he could, but because he had to stop and rest many times, two whole hours went by before they saw the dark outline of the Mourne Mountains against the brightening sky.

At last they arrived at the house, and saw milk bottles on the doorstep.

"The milkman's been!" said Martin Goosegrass in a frightened whisper. "I don't think we're going to be on time. You didn't fly fast enough, Oliver Sundew."

They tumbled through the letter-box – which Mr Nimble Jay had cleverly propped open with a lollipop stick – and flew up the stairs.

"What kept you!" snapped Mr Nimble Jay.

"Never mind, I haven't time to listen. Come
over here, boy, have a look at this tooth. How
are we ever going to get our hands on *that*?"

Pale and beautifully smooth, the perfect
tooth lay at the bottom of an enormous glass of
water.

Toads alive! thought Oliver. It was a long, long way from the top of the water to the bottom of the glass.

"Well? Can you get it?"

"I'll have a go, sir," said Oliver. "Have you got a rope to tie round my waist?"

And now, Oliver Sundew crouched on the rim of the tall-standing glass – and he jumped. His wings twinkled momentarily in the air, then flattened along his back as he dived head first into the water. Down he went – down, down in a stream of bubbles to where the perfect tooth lay like a gorgeous pearl.

Inside the glass and under the water, Oliver felt the air in his lungs running out. It leaked through his lips with a blurble-bubble blurble-bubble noise and shot to the surface of the water like the fizz in lemonade. Roaring winds seemed to blow about his ears, and his heart, instead of beating a nice and steady t-tum, t-tum, felt like it was going tharump, tharump, tharump.

But his hand hit the bottom of the glass. He

touched the tooth and made a fist round it.
Then, as his head began to fill up with light,
he felt the rope tighten at his waist.

Mr Nimble Jay was shouting outside the
glass.

"Heave, get him up there, quick! Has he got
it? Did he get that tooth?"

When Oliver Sundew came out of the water
he looked like something which has been left
out in the rain for a week. It didn't matter. He
held up the tooth for the others to see.

"What a dive!" said Martin Goosegrass,
who was so amazed that his mouth refused to
close.

"Best I ever saw," agreed Mr Nimble Jay.

Cornpepper Rose couldn't help herself. "He
did get it," she yelled. "You are wonderful,
Oliver Sundew," and she immediately danced
a jig with Henry B. They wished that the
Fiddler had been there to play one of his lively
tunes.

It was time to go home. Mr Nimble Jay
wiped up the water which had spilled from

Oliver's wings, and then there was just one thing more to be done. They each took a corner of the shining new 50p coin and dropped it gently into the glass of water.

And then down the stairs they flew, out through the letter-box, up between the telephone wires and away across the Mountains of Mourne into the rising sun.

They never knew how lucky they had been. Only five minutes after they left the house, the postman arrived. He wondered why the letter-box had been propped open with a lollipop stick.

Sam McBratney

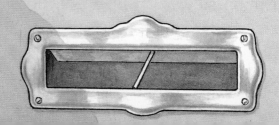